THE
POWER OF
COACHING

Engaging Excellence In Others!

By

Machen MacDonald

With Co-Authors:

- John Assaraf
- Jon Berghoff
- Jim Bunch
- Renate deAngelo
- Harry Hoopis and Joey Davenport
- Mark Rooney
- Brian Tracy
- Brett Bauer
- Don Boyer
- Rich Campe
- Bob Fashano
- Phil Richards
- Jim Rohn
- Diane Ruebling
- Denis Waitley

THE POWER OF COACHING
Engaging Excellence In Others
Published by PLI Publishing
www.ThePowerOfCoaching.com
530-273-8000
Grass Valley, California

Copyright © 2007 ProBrilliance Leadership Institute (PLI)
Library of Congress Control Number: 2007923104
ISBN: 978-1-4243-3125-3

Cover Design by Mick Moore
Killergraffix@cox..net

Editing, Composition, and Typography by Patti McKenna
Pcmckenna6@aol.com

This book is available at quantity discounts for bulk purchase.
For more information, contact:
www.ThePowerOfCoaching.com
Telephone: 530-273-8000
Grass Valley, California

Printed in the United States of America

PRAISE FOR THE POWER OF COACHING

"If you read an inspirational book every month, you'll be a different and far better person one year from now. The Power of Coaching is one such book that can change your life, containing nuggets of wisdom that can reap rewards for many years to come."
Mickey Straub, President
Sales Activity Management, Inc.

"By applying the ideas and concepts in The Power of Coaching you will find yourself getting more out of the people you lead than you ever thought possible. Coaching works! The wisdom in these pages will put you on a one-way path to success and fulfillment. You'll read it cover to cover."
Edward Deutschlander, CLU, CLF
Executive Vice President North Star Resource Group, President-Elect GAMA International

"Yes! Finally, a book that truly helps both the individual and the manager hit new levels of achievement in their business and personal lives. Make no mistake …the coaching wisdom here is brilliant cutting edge…you will be reading this over and over."
Alex Karis, Founder
Peak Performance Unlimited

"Tremendous! The Power of Coaching is a remarkable compilation of best practices from the greats in the industry. Applying just one of these messages will have a dramatic impact in how you lead people.
Kent M. Campbell, Senior VP
AvivaUsa

"Machen MacDonald understands the power of coaching and has assembled a masterpiece of perspectives from all angles of effective coaching. Let him and his co-authors guide you in becoming a great coach."
Louis J. Cassara, CEO
The Cassara Clinic LLC

"Read The Power of Coaching and discover how to gain the clarity you are looking for, then watch your business grow!"
Russ Lane, President
Compass Financial Resources LLC

"Read this book and discover ways to hold your team accountable, have it be fun and get the results you desire."
Troy Lorenz ChFC, CLU, FIC
Managing Partner, Thrivent Financial for Lutherans

"An excellent coach knows that every client is uniquely brilliant and brilliantly unique. Machen MacDonald is such a coach, and now he is once again provoking our natural brilliance by assembling a masterpiece of perspectives from all angles of effective coaching. If you're committed to mastery and excellence, you must read this book and let Machen and his co-authors guide you in becoming a great coach."
Robert Colt, Owner
Acting Success Now and Whole Coaching

TABLE OF CONTENTS

FOREWORD

Roots

Let me share a quick story.... A few years back, I remember sitting with my mentor over lunch while I poured my heart out in frustration. It seemed like no matter how hard I tried, I just could not break through to many of those I was working with and coaching. Like most leaders, I, too, wanted the best for everyone - a panacea attitude, I suppose.

No matter how hard I taught, shared, or even at times attempted to *control* other people's behavior for their own good (sound like someone you know?), it drove me mad wondering why they could not, or would not, apply the messages given to them.

My lunch guest began to laugh, understanding all too well where I was coming from as he leaned into me and whispered this single word... *Roots*.

"What?," I asked.

"Roots," he repeated and went on to tell me something that changed my life and the way I worked with people from that day forward. "It's like this," he said. "When you see someone, let's say they are down and out, even in the gutter, you want to go over and pick them up, dust them off, and get their life in order and send them on their way to a new life of happiness."

"Absolutely!" I shouted back.

"Well, that is why you fail," he responded as he sat back in his chair, taking a sip of coffee.

"I don't get it; I just want to help," I muttered.

"Yes, I understand that – yet, you are missing the key ingredient," said the wiser of us two.

I just sat there, looking like a confused puppy with my head tilted to the side.

"Roots," He continued..."It works like this... first they have to *WANT* your help. Say you find someone who is in need of change - they can even be in the situation you mentioned before, really down and out - only rather than trying to help **everyone** – look for that person who is bleeding from their hands."

"You see, these people are different. Remember, it doesn't matter where people are at, coming from or have been; we've all had hard times in our lives, but its the people who understand the roots philosophy that are the ones who truly end up going from where they are to where they want to be."

I inquired, "Why are they bleeding?"

"Because they don't want to be in that situation any longer." He mentored, "These people are bleeding from their hands because they are reaching out of that place, the metaphorical gutter so to speak, and are grabbing at a hand full of roots and pulling themselves out. Now, rather than waste time attempting to (FIX) everyone as you were doing before, just stand behind those who are reaching for the roots and offer encouraging words and guide them where to grab hold of the next set of roots, and eventually they will do something special and pull THEMSELVES out, and then have the tools to teach others to do the same."

Pretty good advice, huh? I've applied this principle since that time, and I have gone from a 30% success rate with working with people to over 80%! It's a simple golden rule – God helps those who help themselves - and we can be a small factor in his handiwork by simply being the guide.

What you have in your hands is the roadmap of time-tested ideas, suggestions and wisdoms offered by some of today's greatest leaders in personal development.

As you are about to witness for yourself, Machen has compiled a virtual masterpiece of classic inspirations that are simply brilliant. The true test is how we will put these suggestions to work, for ourselves as well as for the betterment of others. Will we continue attempting to help everyone, or will we seek out those who are ready for the transformation? The choice is yours. Mr. MacDonald has given us the tools; now it's up to us to put them to work.

Best wishes and whatever you do….. Keep smilin'…….

Gregory Scott Reid
CEO, WISH Entertainment, Inc.
www.PassItOnToday.com

DEDICATION

T his book is dedicated to you, the reader. This book found you or you became aware of it because you are a leader of people. You are among the chosen few in this world who lead and influence others in living a better life for themselves. This is not a calling to be taken lightly.

It's my belief that you have the toughest job in your industry and, potentially the most rewarding. Rewarding not just financially, but psychically and emotionally, as well, if you allow it.

You help others live more profound lives, and that is admirable. I thank you for your dedication and perseverance, while showing others how to experience more fulfillment and success.

ACKNOWLEDGEMENTS

M y deep love and thanks go to my wife, **Laura;** sons, **Drake** and **Shane;** and daughter, **Adrian,** for allowing me the gift to feel like the world's best husband and father. You continually inspire and amaze me with your love, support and understanding.

To **all our authors** for believing in this project and stepping up and meeting the most demanding of deadlines. Because of your brilliance and contribution, others can learn from your wisdom. It has been an honor and blessing to work with each of you. Together we brought about, in only three short months, a published work that is sure to inspire many. This book is proof of what is possible with vision, focus, and commitment...and some great coaching!

To **Jeff Hughes** for your insights and ideas on how to breathe abundant life into this project.

To **Don Boyer** for being my mentor and shepherd on this project. Your caring, guidance and coaching along this path have been both a gift and a blessing.

To **Patti McKenna** for your brilliant editing and making this a masterpiece. Your dedication is inspiring.

To **Mick Moore** for your creative direction and bringing yet another awesome book design into the world. Your patience went well beyond the call of duty.

To **Diane Ruebling** for your wisdom, inspiration and for opening many doors so we may share our brilliance and help others to get REAL.

To **John Assaraf** for being an awesome example of "having it all" and for sharing "The Secret" with the world. It's an honor to be able to call you a friend.

To **Jim Bunch** for living a happy, healthy, and wealthy life and showing us all how to play and win The Ultimate Game.

To **Denis Waitley** for sharing your psychology of winning and getting me to know that part of me that is here to serve others.

To **Harry Hoopis** for demonstrating what is possible when you are the "Resident Big Thinker" of your organization.

To **Joey Davenport** for being wise beyond your years and playing full out during crunch time.

To **Bob Fashano** for teaching me to listen and showing me the freedom associated with not taking on people's monkeys.

To **Phil Richards** for being a shining example of how, if your values are clear, the decisions are easy. Your generous contribution of time and energy in the final hour is greatly appreciated.

To **Mark Rooney** for challenging me to step up into leadership early in my career. It set the pace for things to come.

To **Jim Rohn** for always challenging me to think bigger.

To **Jon Berghoff** for stepping up and playing your big game and sharing your wisdom on a global scale. It is fun to watch you, Yo Pal Hal and your team impact the lives of others.

To **Rich Campe** for challenging me to play a bigger game and really showing me how to lead with my strengths and live a more fulfilling life. It just keeps getting better!

To **Brett Bauer,** the man of the hour, for having confidence in this project to be a pivotal process in your expansion of taking your practice to the next level. It's an honor.

To **Renate deAngelo** for your upbeat spirit and wonderful contribution to the coaching world.

To **Brian Tracy** for your no-nonsense insights and continued support of the projects I touch.

To **Gregory Scott Reid** for your graceful introduction to Don Boyer and "Passing It On." This book is a direct result of one simple introduction that took root. You impact more lives than you know. Thank you for penning your rousing foreword.

To **God** for all that is, was and ever will be.

INTRODUCTION

I t is said that people don't join organizations, they join people. Nor do they leave organizations, they leave people. This book is intended to make you a more attractive leader to the ideal people you are seeking to join your team. By understanding the wisdom in this book, you will also benefit from knowing how to continually increase your value as a leader so you can lock in higher retention of those you lead. As a manager or leader, you wear many hats, including recruiter, trainer, planner, business consultant, sales professional, and coach, just to name a few.

The ideas, strategies and wisdom that make up this book are from the top leaders in the industry who have built organizations of excellence and have the respect of their peers. One of the most critical skills that sets them apart from the pack is their ability to "coach." They are effective at transporting the people they lead from where they currently are to where their vision becomes a reality. You will learn from their subject matter expertise as it relates to the industry and how they so eloquently integrate the power of coaching to get the results that are demanded in this business.

There is a whole profession dedicated to coaching. In this book you will also learn from the premier master coaches of the coaching world. These coaches understand business. They will share with you strategies on how you can raise your game as a coach. You will discover how to really hold people, including yourself, accountable; how to eloquently challenge people to go the extra mile and reach their potential; how to identify people's strengths and show them how to lead with their strengths and not fall prey to their weaknesses. By mastering the content within the covers of this book, your stock will rise as a leader because you will become aware of what the power of coaching really is. You will become known as a leader who is a great coach who can engage the excellence in those you lead.

Congratulations on taking the first step on the journey to really affecting others profoundly. As you read something you resonate with, take action and learn more about what you are reading and how it can dramatically impact you and your organization. You will also notice that each of the contributing authors has provided their contact information. They welcome your questions and comments.

At The Power Of Coaching, we are always receiving and collecting great and wonderful information, wisdom and strategy from leaders and coaches. If you have something you want to contribute or learn more about, then visit our free website:

www.ThePowerOfCoaching.com

It's up to you to make it happen. Coaching makes the difference. Make it Up, Make it Fun and Make it Happen!

All the best,
Machen MacDonald

Jim Bunch

Jim Bunch is a widely respected coach, speaker, and entrepreneur whose mission is to inspire happiness, health and wealth worldwide through transformational coaching programs, seminars, and products, such as books, CDs, and online courses. He has over 12 years of professional speaking experience and has given more than a thousand presentations on personal and professional development. To stay connected to the latest information, programs, and research in creating happy, healthy, and wealthy lives, be sure to visit Jim at www.jimbunch.com or call 888-335-3880 for more information.

Chapter One

THE ULTIMATE COACH APPROACH TO WINNING

Jim Bunch

What is the purpose of a coach?

If you were to ask 100 CEOs or managers what the purpose of a coach is, you'd probably hear: to inspire, to educate, to empower, to challenge and to instill accountability. All of these would be correct responses; they're all essential elements of the dynamic relationship between coach and client. The bottom line, however, is that the purpose of a coach is to **win**.

Arnold Palmer may have said it best: "Success in golf depends less on strength of body than upon strength of mind and character." Combine this observation with a recent Harvard Business Review statement - The goal of coaching is the goal of good management: to make the most of an organization's valuable resources. Now you have function and purpose for coaching.

Most of us think of coaching and winning in terms of what happens on the field in sports, but winning in business happens at the office, in the boardroom, and in the daily interaction between colleagues and clients.

Essential to winning at the Game of Life, however, is the creation of success both on and *off* of the playing field, in and *out* of work-mode. Real success comes when our professional and personal goals are in-line and supporting one another, as any disconnect between the two creates friction and lack of focus on both fronts.

Corporate coaching finds its roots, not surprisingly, in sports; and we've all encountered coaching and/or mentoring in one form or another. There are many types of coaching and many levels of coaching. We're all accustomed to what I call Sandlot Coaches: parents and friends who coach us on everything from how to walk and talk to how to become successful in life. We grew up with school teachers who coached us both on how and what to learn and preachers who taught us what to believe about God and religion. Our culture and our society also indirectly coach us through the media on how to live and how to navigate our way through our personal and professional life. I call this Sandlot Coaching because its usually free and its usually information that's given to us on every street corner by every person, whether or not they are proven to have mastered that area of life or not.

Then there are the professional coaches, and, for general conversation, they typically fall into one of three categories. The first category of professional coaches have been formally trained to coach others, but in many cases, they have not produced outstanding results in their own lives, even though they may be able to help players become better in certain games.

The second level of coaches have proven track records in whatever the game is they've played. They are teaching what they know based on their experiences and insights into the game, but they don't necessarily have any formal training on how to coach.

Then we have what I call *"The Ultimate Coaches."* These are mentor coaches who have accomplished outstanding results, not only in their professional lives, but they have also created outstanding results personally and have been trained in the art and science of coaching. They share their knowledge and their wisdom with their clients and help their clients to play and win really big games.

So, what's the goal with all of this coaching? In sports, the goal is to win the game, the season, and ultimately the championship. In business, you're out to win financially every quarter and every year. In life, as a whole, you are out to create happiness, health, and wealth…the ultimate winning combination.

What does it take to create a winning team? Well, you either recruit the very best players or you take what you have, train and coach them to be the best that they can be…and help them to become the ultimate players.

In 1999, I was part of a start up team called bamboo.com. The company was started by two gentlemen under the age of 30, and quickly grew from 6 employees to 1,500 employees, then went public after only one year. We quickly became the world leader in virtual tours of homes when we merged with Ipix.com, which is the name the company now goes by. I came on board to help recruit, train and coach the employees so we could have the ultimate team. We were recruiting team members at warp speed, and it became apparent that we had two types of players coming on board. We had "pros" and "Rudys."

"Pros" had already played a big game in other industries and knew how to do whatever it takes to be successful. They had the "winners" mindset and fit right into the high energy, high performance environments we had created... we simply had to align them with the vision and mission of "changing the way the world views real estate," then teach them the basics about virtual tours and off to the races they went.

We also had some managers who had what I called the "Rudy Strategy for hiring." Daniel "Rudy" Ruettiger was a young man who was 5'7" and not that fast, but he had a dream to play college football at Notre Dame. Through perseverance and passion, he finally got a chance to play in one regular season football game. He didn't play on the full-time team, and he was never drafted into the pros, but he had the heart of a lion and with five seconds left in the final game of the season...he got his chance to step onto the field. When you recruit "the Rudys," keep in mind they bring heart to all the players but they require a lot of training and coaching to reach the pros.

My strategy is to recruit great players who already have wins under their belts and evolve them into outstanding leaders so that the entire team wins. There are two schools of thought on how to do this. Some coaches believe that the client has "all the answers inside of them" and that they just need to unearth them. Others feel that the clients "don't know what they don't know," so they need to be shown what to do along the way.

My observation is that most clients do have inherent wisdom about the decisions they should be making in their lives, but there are many occasions when they need specific strategies and skills to accomplish their goals. The job of the coach is to share insights to accelerate their learning. After all, if you are expecting your quarterback to win games but you haven't taught him how to properly hand off the ball, he will eventually figure it out himself, but at what cost to him and the team?

One of the essential steps in coaching is instilling accountability. It is the coach's job to create environments that are conducive to setting the client/players up to win. Doing so will allow the team to play to the strengths of the players and manage the weaknesses. The coach must also be consistent and intentional about enforcing boundaries. This both sets up trust with the client and creates positive expectations that seldom even need to be discussed.

Throughout the coaching process it is essential to continually raise standards, thus, giving the client new levels of greatness to achieve. Such continual growth provides a sort of self-fulfilling prophecy of continued success.

How does a coach help players win?

The key to helping players win is for the coach to quickly assess the player's strengths, skills, and weaknesses and help the players make improvements in three categories.

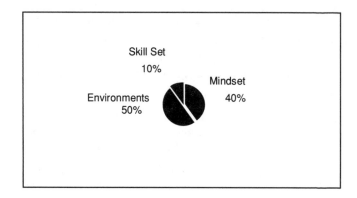

Skill set makes up about 10% of the game. Part of the coach's job is to assess the skills of the player and compare them with the skills necessary to execute the game plan. A game without a plan is a plan to fail, but keep in mind that the game plan must constantly evolve once the game begins.

If you've watched the NFL lately, you will notice the players and their coaches are often on the sidelines reviewing photographs of the last play so that they can make real-time adjustments during the game. Reviewing the game tapes after the game is over is important, but real-time coaching, on the field, during the game, can be the difference between a win and a loss.

Mindset is 40% of the game. Here the player learns to strategize and manage his or her own inner game. Of utmost importance in coaching is helping the client to focus on the wins they are achieving while helping them to visualize their upcoming performances with perfection. Emotional and physical balance are key here, as well. People condition their minds and bodies in different ways. The coach's role in helping the player to find the affirmations and physical activities to accomplish that balance is very important. Last, but not least, a coach must appeal to the player's spiritual sensibilities. Help the player design their internal world (their vision, mission, purpose, values, strengths, etc.) to align with their external game. If the inside world is not aligned with the external game, they can't win consistently and neither will the team. We see this all the time in corporations where the employee's heart isn't into the work and the performance suffers.

A great coach knows intuitively and instinctually how to play to their client's values. These values determine the big picture of the player's life. Within that big picture, it's essential to remember that: people will give you 8 hours a day for a paycheck, 10 hours a day for a job they like, and 16 hours a day for a mission, a team and a coach they believe in!

Environments are the third, and often overlooked, element for success; and they account for up to 50% of the game (some say even more). If the environments are not growing and evolving, the player will not grow and evolve and they will be living in a state of drag (low energy, resistance, slow movement) rather than in a state of inspiration. By designing your environments so they are a constant source of inspiration, you will find your daily habits, actions and goals are much easier to attain, and you will no longer have to rely on "willpower" to get the job done.

One of my personal mentors and coaches, the late Thomas Leonard, who was considered by many to be the founder of coaching, shared with me that the key to long-term change is not willpower...it's the environments. Most people are trying to use willpower to change their behaviors and end up frustrated and overwhelmed. We see this all the time when people go to seminars or read a book on how to change their life and they get pumped and motivated, but the moment they return home, they slip back into the same habits. That's because willpower, like the ability to focus, is a mental faculty and it's only on when you turn it on. Environments, however, are on 24 hours a day, 7 days a week.

You've probably heard that "people are a by-product of their environments," or stated another way, "you are who you spend the most time around."

For example, if you grew up in the USA, you would speak a different language, have different beliefs and different behaviors than if you grew up in the Middle East. These environments are so powerful in shaping who we are that people with different beliefs are willing to kill each other over their differences. This is because we are all programmed and conditioned by the environments. The challenge is that most people are unaware of the impact the environments are having on them and they are unaware of the nine environments that are always programming us.

The best athletes in the world play at a higher level when they are around other world class athletes. The same is true for the corporate player. The better the team, the better the player will become. The key is to craft environments that inspire the players to play their ultimate games.

The following is a snapshot of the Nine Environments of You. To learn more about this coaching tool, visit CoachVille.com, one of the leading schools for training coaches.

The Nine Environments of YOU!

Self · Spiritual · Body · Memetic · Nature · YOU! · Relationships · Physical · Network · Financial

Copyright 2005 CoachVille LLC

A Snapshot of the Environments

You
The core of you that is unchanging

Memetic
Beliefs, Ideas, Knowledge, Cultural Norms,
Frameworks

Body
Physical Body, Health, Energy

Self
Personality, Gifts, Talents, Strengths, Emotions

Spiritual
Connection to a Higher Source, Love and Self

Relationships
Family, Friends, Close Colleagues, Support Personnel

Network
Community, Strategic Partners, Customers

Financial
Money, Investments, Budgeting, Insurance

Physical
Home, Office, Furnishings, Equipment / Technology

Nature
Outdoors, Beauty, Seasons, Cycle of Life

Teaching someone what to do, or just giving them more information will not work long term. If more information were the key, wouldn't every librarian be wealthy?

To create sustainable change, the environments around the player must evolve so their behaviors change. People are a byproduct of their environments. The old way of reaching goals is to try to use force and willpower to "push" your way to your goals. The coach's job is to create environments that reflect and support the desired behaviors and to literally "pull the players" into their goals. Which do you think is easier and more likely to be successful, "pushing" or being "pulled"?

By crafting your "ultimate environments," you will achieve your goals effortlessly, efficiently and effectively. You will no longer have to rely on willpower to get the job done, and you will stop relying on yourself to complete your goals. If well designed, your environments will become your partners in your goal achievement.

What are the consequences of not having well designed environments?

You will be living by default rather than by design, which causes emotional, mental and physical reactions, which can increase stress. You will find that you are constantly in struggle and friction with your environment. Life just does not flow freely without well designed environments. You will find that you are lacking the inspiration required to get the job done (you will be relying more on willpower than flow to move forward).

What does it take to become the Ultimate Coach?

When you are the Ultimate Coach, you, by the very nature of your game, turn your players into leaders. You accomplish this by having a compelling purpose to your game, one that people are drawn to and want to incorporate into their own lives. As the Ultimate Coach, you must also raise your own standards and up the ante in your own game. Doing so will make your game the driving force in your life because it will also be your passion. And, of course, you must become a professional. One of my favorite lines comes from a car commercial by General Motors…"Amateurs practice until they get it right; professionals practice until they can't get it wrong."

Until we connect again, have fun and Create your Ultimate Life!!!

Jim Bunch

The Ultimate Life Coach and Entrepreneur

For more inspiration and to learn how to become the ultimate player and to win The Ultimate Game of Life…visit us at www.JimBunch.com, *where we turn players into leaders.*

Special offer: Go to **www.JimBunch.com** and sign up for our complimentary podcast "Secrets of the Masters" where we interview world leaders in the areas of Happiness, Health, and Wealth.

Harry Hoopis

Joey Davenport

Harry Hoopis, CLU, ChFC is the CEO and Joey Davenport, CLTC is Executive Director of Development for *Hoopis Performance Network* based in Chicago, Illinois. Harry was inducted in the GAMA International Management Hall of Fame and is a contributing author to *The Essentials of Management Development.* Joey, a Certified Trainer and Master Coach, is the Executive Producer of *Enduring Relationships* and the *Hoopis University.* The *Hoopis Performance Network* provides field-tested tools and resources for organizational leaders and sales producers in the financial services arena. With over 30 years of industry-leading experience, these proven resources have been created and enhanced in their very own "living laboratory." They can be contacted at www.hoopisnetwork.com or by sending an email to info@hoopisnetwork.com. They may be reached by telephone at (847) 663-7770.

Chapter Two

ENGAGING EXCELLENCE
THROUGH EXPECTATIONS

Harry Hoopis and Joey Davenport

P erhaps one of the best known speeches ever given in our industry was delivered by Albert E. Gray, an official of the Prudential Insurance Company, at the National Association of Life Underwriters convention in 1940. Gray stated, "The common denominator of success, the secret of success of every person who has ever been successful, lies in the fact that they have formed habits of doing things that failures don't like to do."

In reading his speech, you will find there is a lot more to his profoundness than just the oft-quoted line about habits. He went on to describe what those things are that people don't like to do. Gray says that all those things we don't like to do emanate from this one basic dislike particular to our type of selling. We don't like to call on people who don't want to see us, to talk about something they don't want to talk about. Gray says any reluctance to follow a definite prospecting program, to use prepared sales talks, to organize time and to organize effort are all caused by this one basic dislike.

Gray states, "We've got to realize, right from the start, that success is something that is achieved by the minority of people, and is, therefore, unnatural and not to be achieved by following our natural likes or dislikes, nor by being guided by our natural preferences and prejudices." He explains that people are creatures of habit just as machines are creatures of momentum. If you do not deliberately form good habits, then unconsciously you will form bad ones. Every single qualification for success is acquired through habit.

These principles hold as true in our business today as they did back in 1940. So, as organizational leaders and coaches, our role is to help our advisors form the habit of doing the things unsuccessful people simply are not willing to do. Therefore, we have to create an environment of excellence based upon clearly defined expectations, and then we must reinforce these expectations by holding advisors accountable through ongoing coaching and development systems. These expectations should be objective, measurable, clearly communicated, and also agreed upon. In addition, organizational leaders should also establish clearly defined rewards and consequences for each expectation. This is critically important because expectations without consequences are merely suggestions.

So, why is accountability so important to an advisor's success? Well, most of us know intellectually what we need to do on a daily basis to be successful. However, our primitive nature is wired to follow the path of least resistance and tends to gravitate towards that which is most pleasing. So, we have to set up our environment to force us to follow through with our commitments by establishing good work habits. The framework of this environment is ongoing development and supervision systems. The coach simply facilitates this process along the way.

There are two basic types of coaching incorporated throughout this process: Directive and Collaborative. Directive Coaching is a relationship in which the coach prescribes a specific solution to a specific problem. This type of coaching is utilized when an advisor's problem is easily identified, for example, if someone is not achieving certain activity expectations, is disorganized, or consistently tardy. Collaborative Coaching is a relationship in which the coach primarily asks questions to allow the advisor to draw their own conclusions and learn through self-discovery. This type of coaching is utilized the majority of the time; however, a good coach can effectively blend the two coaching styles when appropriate.

Once clearly defined expectations and rewards/ consequences have been established by your leadership team, you must then create your coaching and development systems. Based on our experience, these systems should incorporate daily, weekly, monthly and quarterly "touch points."

Our coaching and development systems include the following components:

Daily Activity Coaching

The first component we focus on is daily activity coaching. We know the habits formed in the first 90 days in the business will typically remain with an advisor throughout their career. Therefore, this is a very important time in a new advisor's career and warrants daily coaching and supervision. These daily activity coaching sessions are typically 15 minutes in length and take place for the first 90 days.

The purpose of these sessions is twofold: to provide support and to challenge. The activity coach should provide support when the new advisor needs encouragement or is achieving the expectations that have been established. The coach should challenge the new advisor when they are not meeting expectations or not achieving the activity levels they need to become successful.

The meeting involves discussing the previous day's activity, determining what is working well, what is not working so well, and what additional help the advisor needs from the leadership team. This meeting also includes an inspection of any fact finders that were taken during the previous day. We refer to this as "inspecting what you expect."

These sessions typically involve Directive Coaching until the advisor begins to "grasp" the business, then the coach can move to more of a collaborative approach. This empowers the new advisor to begin to solve his or her issues by themselves.

Weekly Mentoring and Joint Field Work

In addition to daily activity coaching, each advisor should also meet with a coach one time per week to discuss more in-depth issues pertaining to the business. During these sessions, the coach and advisor will typically work on sales skills, case preparation, business development issues and goal setting. These coaching sessions are much more collaborative and should consist of the coach guiding the advisor to their own solutions. A major role of the coach in these sessions is to analyze the advisor's activity patterns to assess areas of improvement either around sales skills or sales process.

The new advisor should also be required to conduct joint work in the field with the assigned coach, as well as various members of the organization who are positive role models. This enables the new advisor to observe various styles so they can begin to adapt their own unique style. In addition, it provides an opportunity for the new advisor to "shadow" veteran advisors so they can acquire practical field experience and receive feedback.

Weekly and Monthly Clientbuilder Study Groups

A major part of our culture is weekly and monthly Clientbuilder Study Groups. In the first twelve months in the business, each new advisor is required to attend weekly peer accountability sessions. During these 30-minute sessions, each new advisor reports on their activity from the previous week. They also discuss what is working well and what is not working so well in their business. They receive feedback from their peers in the form of challenge and support. These sessions are followed by weekly training and education sessions.

In addition, every advisor in our organization participates in a monthly Clientbuilder Study Group (even 30 year veterans!). During these monthly sessions, advisors meet for three to four hours with a group of their peers who are at similar production levels. Each advisor reports on their activity from the previous month, as well as what is going on in their business. After reporting, the advisor then receives feedback from the group in the form of challenge or support. We equate these groups to having your own personal "Board of Advisors." These peer accountability groups are woven into the fabric of our culture and have become a major catalyst to us obtaining organizational excellence.

Quarterly Coaching Sessions

Each quarter, all advisors meet with the Managing Partner. During these quarterly coaching sessions, the Managing Partner reviews the advisor's goals, as well as the progress they have made toward these goals. These coaching sessions are primarily collaborative, with the Managing Partner focused on getting the advisors to think "bigger" about their business. These sessions also provide an opportunity for the advisor to receive feedback or advice in regards to any personal issues they may be dealing with such as family, finances, etc.

In conclusion, once we have recruited advisors into this business, we have to fulfill our promise that we will provide them with the coaching and development necessary to become successful. This is a simple business, but not an easy business. It's simple in the fact that we know what we need to do on a daily basis to become successful. It's not easy in the fact that we have to continue to consistently do those things day in and day out. This business is not about success; it is about sustainability. Without ongoing coaching and development, sustainability becomes impossible. Ultimately, our job as organizational leaders and coaches is to create an environment of expectations and accountability which will help people grow and continue to grow: personally, professionally and financially.

Machen MacDonald

Machen MacDonald, CPCC, CCSC is the creator of The Power of Coaching book series and the founder of the ProBrilliance Leadership Institute. With over 15 years of experience in the financial services industry, he's now a full time coach dedicated to showing business leaders how to provoke their brilliance so they can experience their ideal life. He's an accomplished author, as well as a highly sought after speaker for his dynamic and unique perspectives on achieving success in all areas of life. Machen resides on his ranch in Northern California with his wife and their three children. Contact Machen at (530) 273-8000.

Chapter Three

EIGHT STEP E.A.G.L.E.
(EMPOWERING ANGLE GOAL LEVERAGING EXERCISE)

Machen MacDonald

I t is said that we may not always be able to control our circumstances or the situations within which we find ourselves. However, we always have the power to choose the healthiest perspective from which to view what is going on. Choosing the healthiest perspective or finding the most empowering angle on something may not always be easy in the face of adversity or disappointment. People who seem to gravitate toward success and fulfillment on a regular basis have mastered the ability to locate and operate from the most empowering angle, regardless of the state of affairs.

Forming the habit of perpetually finding the most empowering angle from which to view a given set of circumstances can be the single most effective skill you possess. Having this skill will set you apart from the rest of the pack. You will be able to soar with the eagles and command respect and admiration that others can only dream about.

In this eight-step coaching model, you will learn to coach yourself, as well as those you lead, to live more in alignment with your purpose, values and goals, thereby getting greater results in less time.

To affect desired change, it is critical to align awareness, action and accountability. The EAGLE 8 provides you that alignment. Let's dive in:

1. Identify and label your point of view

Name how you feel about your situation. For example, you may feel stuck, cornered, off-track, bummed, or overwhelmed. Identify and name your personal point of view. At first, you may not even recognize it as a perspective. However, if you are saying things like, "It's just a fact of life," "That's just the way it is," or "It's out of my control," then you are probably experiencing a situation or area of your life in which you are stuck. This, of course, is only a single, less-than-empowering, point of view. In fact, what you are experiencing is your current perspective on how you are viewing life. It is simply the angle from which you are seeing what is. Just as a diamond has many facets and you can't see all of them at any one time, the same is true for events and circumstances.

You may tell yourself things like, "There just isn't enough time to do it all; I never have enough time; or, Why do I always run out time?" It's not that there is not enough time; you are simply seeing the angle of there not being enough time. There are many other angles. Here are a few: Time exists so I don't have to do it all at once; all there is, is time; I manage my time wisely and get the important things done on time.

You must come to realize that your current experience is a result of your angle on things. In quantum physics, it is said that whatever you say to yourself before you look at something, determines what you see. Therefore, choose wisely the angle you desire for your viewing pleasure.

So, Step One is simply giving your current perspective a label. By asking yourself, "How am I choosing to look at this current situation?" or, "Where am I coming from?" you will identify and be able to name your current perspective.

My current angle is:_____.

2. Identify other more empowering perspectives.
You will want to explore the other facets that exist. Ask yourself, "What's another way to look at the situation? How would I like to be able to look at it? Or, how would somebody who could easily handle this look at this situation?" Imagine what their perspective might be. Perhaps, that may be one you would like to adopt.

Repeat this step a few times to come up with different angles on how to better view the setting. Brainstorm and create a list of three or more of them here:

1._____
2._____
3._____

3. Try them on.

Now that you have identified a number of different, more empowering angles from which to approach your circumstances, you must choose the one that will serve you best.

Here is how you can be sure to choose the best one for you.

Step into each of these possible perspectives so you can experience it and make a determination of which will serve you best. Remember, you can always go back to where you started. I am not here to take anything away from you. I am here to help broaden your horizons, provoke you to discover what's really inside of you, and play *big*! Are you ready?

Choose one of your new perspectives. Really get into it. Get up if you are sitting, and move to another place in the room. This will change your immediate, physical perspective and support the change in your mental perspective. When you are ready, take in a big breath and embrace this *new* perspective. Imagine what it is like living from this perspective. Breathe as if *you are the essence of your chosen new perspective and feel how different this new perspective feels.* Use your imagination and stand as if you know in your bones you can operate from this new angle. Move as if; really feel as if. Picture the situation as if. How do you feel about the situation now that you're viewing it from this new angle? Good? Excellent!

Okay...shake it out. Let go of that perspective, and try on one of the other perspectives you came up with. Not later. Right now! Come on... When you are ready, take in a big *new* breath and embrace this *new* perspective. Keep doing this for each of the empowering angles you came up with.

I am proud of you for going for it on this one. You'll be glad you did. If you feel you need to try on some other perspectives, go for it! If you feel you have found one that works for you, then we can move on.

4. Choose Your Most Empowering Perspective.
From Step Three, notice which perspective contributed to your energy level the most. Take that perspective and, once again, embrace that perspective you have chosen for yourself. When you are ready, consume a big *new* breath and embrace this perspective. Imagine what it is like living from this perspective. Breathe as if you are the essence of *your chosen new perspective and feel how different this desired perspective feels.* Use your imagination and stand as if you know in your bones you have achieved what you want and everything is working out the way you want it to. Move as if; really feel as if. Picture the situation as if. How do you feel about the situation now? Now double that feeling. Good! Now magnify it by ten! Spend a little extra time picturing the situation from this perspective. See a direct and clear path between you and having what you want. It is available to you to be had. Now, by practicing this perspective, you are making yourself available to it!

Only four more steps….stay with me.

5. Create a plan that addresses the situation.

From your new perspective, begin with the end in mind. See yourself having achieved your desired results. Know you achieved this through living and coming from this new perspective. Now that you have it, work backwards.

What are the actions you have taken? What are the feelings and emotions that propelled you to take those actions? What were the thoughts and beliefs you formed in order to feel those feelings that propelled you to take those actions?

Take your answers to these questions and script your plan. Remember a good plan today is far better than a best plan tomorrow. Do this now! Write something down now! The power is in the now!

6. Commit to the plan and to yourself.

Keep reminding yourself that this is your game and you make the rules. This can be easy, or it can be hard. You decide. You must commit. There is a difference between being committed to your success and just interested in your success. When you are interested, you do what you must do when it is convenient for you. When you are committed, you do what you must do when it must be done. There is no better time than right now. You are either committed to achieving what you want or you are not. Which is it? There is no in between. Hurl yourself at that which you desire, and the universe will bring it to you.

Now comes the acid test. Be aware, you may have to say "No" to some things in order to achieve what you want, and you may need to say "Yes" to certain things, as well.

In order to achieve _____, I am willing to say "**NO**" to the following:

1._____

2._____

3._____

And I am willing to say "**YES**" to the following:

1._____

2._____

3._____

We have come a long way in expanding your list of options, choosing a perspective, and creating a plan. Are you willing to commit to do what it takes to have what is yours in your life? Since the answer is a resounding "*YES*," I want you to imagine a line on the ground. When you are ready to commit to the plan and say "*yes!*" to the key elements and "*no!*" to the distractions, step across the line.

Once you cross the line, you will notice a shift in your being. This is powerful. Let's keep the momentum going.

7. Take action.

This should actually feel easy to do compared to all the work you just performed. From your plan, select one item. The action can be as simple as setting a new time on your alarm clock or saying "no" to excuses...others' as well as your own. Chances are you are so pumped up at the shift within you that you want to do a lot more. That's great! Go for it! Do something, anything, to forward the action.

Will this empowering tidal wave of emotion last forever? It may or may not. Might you slip off track in a week or two? Perhaps. When you feel the empowering emotion fading, remember to find your perspective and fully connect with it all over again just as you did in Step Four. Set up your environment to empower you. Play your favorite music; smell your favorite scents. If you love the outdoors, be there. While in your best possible environment, review your action plan for a couple minutes each day, fully engaged from your desired perspective.

8. Be accountable.

Make a commitment to a coach or an accountability buddy that you will do certain key actions within your plan by a certain date. We may break a commitment to ourselves, but we usually won't break commitments with others so easily. Here is an example of how accountability works. Let's say you commit to walking for 40 minutes at 6:30 a.m. every other day. You do it the first couple of times, and then there is that one morning when the warm sheets feel too good. Rather than rolling out of bed, you want to roll over in bed.

You rationalize that it's only one day, and it's no big deal. And then one day turns into one week, and then one month, and finally you are no better off than when you started.

Alternatively, having decided to be accountable, you find a friend or colleague who also wants to walk, and you commit to walking with them on a regular schedule. Now when the alarm rings, you get up and go because you don't want to let your buddy, Bill, down. Maybe you even made a side bet with Bill that the first one to not show up for the walk owes the other one $500. Are you getting it? Find and create a structure that works to motivate or even trick you into doing the behavior you ultimately must do to get the desired result.

In a nutshell, here is the 8 Step EAGLE:

1. Identify and name your current angle of how you are seeing what is.
2. Identify more empowering perspectives.
3. Try them on.
4. Choose a new perspective that will serve you better.
5. Create a plan from your new perspective.
6. Commit to the plan and to yourself.
7. Take action.
8. Be accountable.

Commit to developing this as a new habitual way of thinking, and you will be in awe at how fast you can affect desired change in yourself and others.

Diane M. Ruebling

 Diane M. Ruebling is the President of The Ruebling Group LLC, a company that provides executive coaching, business planning and performance systems. In addition to her professional career, Diane has held a variety of public service roles. The most current is a Presidential appointment to the Board of Directors for the Overseas Private Investment Corporation (OPIC). She is married to her husband, Charles, and has two children. To contact Diane, email her at diane@rueblinggroup.com or telephone her at 801-520-6761. To find our more about the Ruebling Group, visit their website at www.rueblinggroup.com.

Chapter Four

LEVERAGING PEERS *AND* PEER ACCOUNTABILITY...

THE UNTAPPED MINE OF TRANSFORMATIONAL POSSIBILITIES

Diane M. Ruebling

W hen leaders think of coaching, most think of what they, as a leader, want or need to impart to their direct reports. Occasionally, they even consider hiring a coach to work with one of their "stars" or "problems." However, few think of leveraging peers to work with peers as a way for coaching to occur. Leveraging peers and peer accountability is often an organization's untapped mine of transformational possibilities!

It isn't that organizations haven't tried to leverage peers. Historically we have seen quality circles, study groups, project teams, and even staff meetings all having the intent of leveraging the expertise of the individuals in the groups. All of these approaches have their merits, but all too frequently, they fall short of the mark in terms of getting the results desired.

Let's look at another way to leverage peers as coaches. It is called *Action Learning.* This peer-based approach achieves great bottom-line results, as well as enhances personal development. Action Learning is a highly structured, facilitated process of inquiry. The inquiry leads to specific commitments, execution of those commitments, and experiential learning. The capacity of peers to coach peers and to hold each other accountable can literally transform individuals, teams, and even organizations.

Before I describe this amazing process, let me share a story which will illustrate what I mean by transformational possibilities. For years, I had worked in a corporate human resources department of a large financial services firm. After working with some senior field leaders on a major reengineering initiative, they convinced me to "go to the field." My first position was Field Vice President for 47 veteran advisors. I had some significant baggage to overcome....being a woman, from the home office, who had never sold a product. I am sure the advisors thought someone was delusional to send me to be their leader!

It was no secret that to be successful I had to get results, and it was already a fairly successful group of advisors. I knew that I didn't have a lot of technical expertise, but I was confident that I knew a lot about systems, group processes, and leadership development. Knowing that I needed to leverage the expertise of the advisors and what I knew best, I initiated Action Learning Teams.

A key concept in the creation of the teams was to get each advisor to think of themselves as the CEO of their own practice. I knew that I needed to get them to personally own results and have a desire to grow and learn in this role as CEO. Another key concept was to have the advisors believe in an abundance mentality, not a scarcity mentality, so that we could leverage their expertise with each other. Using the Action Learning model, we got 30% growth that first year with 47 veteran advisors, and the next year, with an even bigger territory and over 150 veteran advisors, we achieved 20% growth. I use the word "we," not "I," because it was leveraging the peers, in this case advisors, to share expertise in a meaningful way and to hold each other accountable for execution of commitments that got the results.

Since then, I have used this process with many peer groups of financial advisors, as well as leaders. This past year, an Action Learning team of leaders ended the year achieving the number 1, 2, and 3 spots on their company scorecard. Action Learning works!

So, what is this magical Action Learning process? Well, first of all, it isn't magical. It is a highly structured, facilitated process that, when implemented well, can produce transformational changes for all in the group. The "ah-ha's" and the experiential learning can feel magical, but it doesn't happen without a clear framework for implementation. It requires a strong facilitator for the group who plays a critical role in setting up the team, facilitating the process, as well as communicating key results, reports and logistics. Here are the major components of a good peer Action Learning Team.

Group Formation: Deciding whom to invite to participate on an Action Learning team is important. Following are some critical findings from my experiences with forming a team.

1. Individuals have to choose to participate; they can't be forced or retrofitted into a group.

2. Team members do need to be peers. The peers can be in operations, sales, or in leadership roles.

3. Many times, creating a discrete opportunity which limits the number of people who can be considered for an Action Learning team and having specific criteria to participate are powerful attractors. For instance, with a team of financial advisors, they may have to be at a certain level of production to qualify to participate in an Action Learning team.

4. Be clear ahead of time regarding requirements for a team member's time and personal commitments.

5. All team members must have a business plan with objectives that they are trying to achieve. The plan needs to be concise and clear. I highly recommend a strong, focused one-page plan.

6. The team needs to participate in a kick-off meeting where they are trained in the Action Learning process and where they establish the team's

guiding principles. At that time, everyone shares their business plan and progress on goals year to date.

7. The size of the team differs if you are meeting in person, face to face or virtually on the phone and web. It also varies depending on the amount of time allotted for the meetings and their frequency. A good rule of thumb for monthly meetings is 90 minutes for a virtual meeting and 4 to 6 members on a team. If you meet for 2 plus hours once a month face to face, you can have up to 8 members.

Action Learning Meeting Prep: In an Action Learning meeting, there is one team member who is the "focus team member" of the meeting. It is essential to have the facilitator spend time with that team member prior to the meeting. During this time, the business plan is reviewed and two to three critical bottlenecks are identified. An operating assumption is that everyone has bottlenecks that prohibit or impede their ability to achieve all their objectives for the year or they have opportunities to take success to an even higher level. People always benefit from the discussion on what their most critical bottlenecks are at that point in time. It gives them a chance to stand back and take a good look at the big picture. You want this discussion to happen before the Action Learning team meeting so that time with the team is more focused on addressing a bottleneck versus identifying what it is.

Action Learning Agenda Components: To facilitate the Action Learning process, a consistent agenda where expectations are clear expedites the process. Here are the components I have found to be beneficial:

1. Overall business results review for the whole team.

2. Specific business results review for the focus team member.

3. Identification of the most critical bottlenecks by the focus team member and selection of one to use in the Action Learning process.

4. Action Learning process of inquiry where team members question the focus team member from a extensive list of questions regarding:

   • Getting the facts and objective data.
   • Defining the emotional or cultural filters.
   • Creating future possibilities or "what if's."
   • Deciding specific actions that the focus team member is willing to commit to doing to address the bottleneck between this meeting and the next.

5. Although the majority of the Action Learning meeting is guided by the questioning process, there is an opportunity for the other team members to provide some laser-focused suggestions or recommendations before the commitments are made by the focus team member. This is done after the questioning so that the focus team member has his/her own thoughts and ideas to incorporate with others.

6. The focus team member from the previous meeting reports back on what worked, what didn't work, and what they are willing to do going forward. This is where the experiential learning happens, not only for the focus team member, but for the whole team!

7. Process review by the team on how well they implemented Action Learning and how well they adhered to the teams guiding principles.

Action Learning Follow Up: As you can see in Item 6 on the agenda components, follow up on commitments is a critical part of the process. Immediately after the meeting, the focus team member is sent a form articulating the action steps that he/she committed to implement between this meeting and the next. This commitment to action with peers is incredibly powerful. People will often break commitments to themselves or even their leader, but rarely do they break commitments to their peers. Peer accountability is a wonderful way to move good intentions to great execution!

Awareness, Alignment, Action, and Accountability: With Action Learning, peers can help peers to have a greater *awareness* of what they are trying to achieve. It helps to assure and clarify that their focus is in *alignment* with achieving their objectives. Their *actions* are then derived from a guided process of peer inquiry that leads to commitments. Execution of those commitments and *accountability* to the team of peers gets results and experiential learning. Transformational possibilities are there for you and your team of peers!

Brett Bauer

 Brett Bauer is the owner of Bauer Capital Management, a wealth advisory firm located in Eden Prairie, MN. Brett has been in the insurance and securities business for nearly twenty years. At Bauer Capital Management Brett works primarily with high income, high net worth, self-employed individuals. His team of experts at Bauer Capital allows them to provide their clients with the ability to "get it all" from their firm. Brett and Bauer Capital Management are affiliated with Woodbury Financial Services of Woodbury, MN. Brett can be reached by email at brett@bauercap.com.

Chapter Five

THE COACH WITHIN...

Brett Bauer

I had been working with a coach for several months and finally had my "BIG GAME," as he liked to call it, worked out. It was more difficult than a typical goal-setting session where you state your goal, the timeline and then set out to accomplish it. This time, it was different. I had never worked with a professional coach before, and I felt the whole process of goal setting shouldn't be too difficult. Already that year, my production was over $1.1 Million. I operated under the philosophy of READY, FIRE, now AIM.

With the establishment of my "Big Game," my whole world turned upside down. With the help of my coach, I was excited like never before. Here is my Big Game:

"Generate $2.5MM GDC by the end of 2007, while positioning my practice for sale and developing an exit strategy *so that* - I have more time to spend with my family, golf and support my charitable interests. To that end:

1) I will establish a private foundation that benefits my three primary areas of interest, preventing

drug/alcohol abuse in children, developing a cure for diabetes and educating children about other cultures.

2) Define my role in the business and stick to a schedule.

3) Use my love of golf and club membership as a way to create additional business and opportunity."

My world was turned upside down because, under my coach's guidance, I had to ask myself, hard, provocative questions - questions aimed at getting to the truth of what I wanted out of my life and my business. I was thinking of these things as I prepared a 20-page business plan, taking into account how I wanted my business to continue to grow while meeting my "Big Game."

As I was completing the business plan, I began thinking about my coaching experience so far. My coach had been asking me some very thought-provoking questions.

It reminded me of when I was having a difficult time in a relationship and sought the help of an expert to resolve my relationship problems. It was 1992, and I was in the business of selling life insurance, but considered my real calling as that of an entrepreneur. I had attempted to start two businesses over the past three years, but each time it looked like I might be successful, success was snapped from my grasp, life around me crumbled, and I would have "relationship" problems.

Getting ready to wrap up our meeting, my psychiatrist said to me, "Brett, I think I see a pattern emerging in your life. If you stop drinking, you begin to become successful. If you start drinking, you screw up. Let me say that differently, if you stop drinking, you become successful; if you start, you screw up... So, let me ask you a question: Do you want to be successful, or do you want to be a screw up?"

Good question...of course, the psychiatrist wasn't quite so gentle with me and picked words that stung more like a two-by-four across the face, even suggesting I might be an alcoholic.

"I was afraid you were going to say that," I said. I didn't think I was a drunk, but his verbalization had made me face the fear. In my mind, alcoholics were drunks. I wasn't a drunk. However, it was the cold hard truth. I had made an appointment to fix a relationship problem that I was having. I did not make an appointment to find out that I was the problem.

With my newfound awareness, I voluntarily went into treatment. It was time to become accountable for all of my past actions if I was going to change the future. As of today, I have been sober nearly fifteen years.

The psychiatrist gave me the strength and courage to look at what I wanted to do - be successful - and he had just given me the first step. He told me he knew I could do it. I have never forgotten him, our conversation or the impact he had on my life with those simple words. I believed that I could do it; and, more importantly, I believed in myself. I am forever grateful.

I entered the brokerage industry in April, 1999, and was fortunate to experience the end of a fantastic run-up in the market and its subsequent collapse. I ended 2001 in the hospital with six kidney stones, two very large and four smaller ones. I was off work with no income for the first two months of 2002, and ended up barely taking home over $25,000 in the last twelve months with my broker dealer. If it hadn't been for my wife and her salary, we never would have made it. Our home almost went into foreclosure, and we had to scramble to get caught up. I felt defeated and pretty close to being a failure.

I was beginning to figure out what I wanted out of life, and, more importantly, what I didn't. My wife was counting on me, and I had nearly let her down. With renewed awareness of what I needed to do, I worked harder than I ever had to bring us back from the brink of financial ruin.

I aligned myself with an independent broker dealer in July, 2002. After twelve months, I discovered that I needed to think like a business owner. In October, 2003, I met with a business banker to apply for a line of credit so I could grow the business. Upon completing an analysis for him, I learned a very important thing. I had two types of clients: doctors and small hospitals. The yearly average revenue was virtually identical, and I loved working with both client types. However, there was one significant difference; it took approximately eighteen months for a hospital to become a client, compared to two months for doctors. I had been focusing on hospitals because it appealed to my ego since I was one of the few who really understood the complex financial operations of a hospital. I had invested a great deal of time and energy into learning about hospitals and wasn't willing to stop what I was doing because I loved the challenge they presented and the mental gymnastics they offered. I almost challenged myself out of the business!

Throughout the year, Danelle and I had been investigating our options for adoption. We had learned earlier in the fall that we had been matched and were awaiting the birth of our son. We finally met Jack in December, 2003.

When I saw Jack for the first time in the hospital nursery at two hours old, my heart melted and I cried. He was our son, our child, and the impact of seeing him at that moment changed me. I let go of a lot of emotional baggage; none of it mattered compared to our son. It is hard to imagine unless you have had a child yourself, but it changes you and makes you want to be even better than you ever thought you could.

Upon arriving home with our family, I thought about my discussion with the banker and ways to grow the business. I decided I would attempt to validate my thought processes by talking with several of my best clients to get their thoughts.

As a result, one thing became perfectly clear: What I thought was best for my clients was way off the mark. I asked myself the question, "Why should I continue if what I was doing wasn't working?"

Then, one of my best clients shared an idea with me. I was listening and heard what he said. I was able to figure out from our conversation that this would be something of value to him and others.

"Brett," he started, "I know five doctors who would be interested in making an investment in something like that. In fact, I would be willing to invest more money into something like that!"

Boy, was I stunned! My client had just given me the names of five people and told me he had more money to invest in something that wasn't even available for sale. That conversation provided me with the impetus for growth that propelled my business forward.

During the past year, I have been able to distinguish myself by placing in the top five representatives of a nationally recognized broker dealer.

My wife underwent a kidney transplant on August 4th of this past year. Around the same time, my broker dealer's national sales conference was being held in the Twin Cities area. I was compelled to attend the national sales conference, but I did not want to leave my wife. Her parents were staying with us throughout the transplant process. I was at home, wanting to go to two sessions at the conference; but I knew that as soon as I left, I would be thinking of nothing but being at home with her. Finally, my wife and her mother told me to go, since there was nothing that I would be able to do for her.

It was during that National Sales Conference that I learned of Rich Campe. He has since become my coach. Rich has taught me that people throughout my life have served as coaches. I wasn't always willing to listen and be receptive to the message. When I finally did, each person appeared at a critical point in life and pushed me through to the next one.

For a long time, I looked at success as simply being sober and having a better life because of it. Over time, my definition of success changed; and it didn't feel like life was getting any easier. I didn't feel financially successful until I had been sober for almost twelve years. Business had finally taken off, and it was directly attributable to people who have served as inspirations and coaches.

My business banker helped me to understand my business and learn how to maximize revenues. As much as I loved the challenge and prestige I felt from knowing more about hospitals than others in my business, it was easy to see I was focused on the wrong thing and not getting the result I wanted.

My son, Jack, taught me the importance of letting go and loving. I was able to care on a deeper level, and Jack became a symbol of new beginnings. He gave me the strength and the courage to work smarter, harder and to never quit.

The conversation with my client opened up my mind to other possibilities. As it turned out, I was completely unaware of what my clients thought. When I asked for the information, I was given an opportunity. By the way, my client is the older brother to the psychiatrist I went to solve my "relationship" problems.

It would take a book to describe my life with Danelle and the impact she has had on me. I will simply say I am lucky and grateful to have her in my life. I will always love her. My wife is probably the best coach I have; many times, she has reminded me that it was usually her who had first pointed something out to me. If only I had learned to pay attention.

And, finally, we have my formal coach, Rich Campe. Rich has been my mirror. He allows me to see all the potential that exists in me. I have been fortunate to have people ask me provocative questions that have forced me to face the hard truth. The awareness provided me with the tools to keep asking questions which enable me to coach myself throughout life.

I have learned two things coaching with Rich. First, I would have hit all of the goals I had planned for myself over the next five to ten years. However, because of Rich's thought-provoking questions, ability to help me seek the truth, and skill at finding clarity of purpose, I have aligned my goals so that they are consistent with each other and my life purpose. Now, I will most likely attain all of them in the next one to two years.

Secondly, since Rich has mobilized me and accelerated me along my path, I wonder what would have happened if I had met Rich sooner, say ten or fifteen years ago, when I first acknowledged that I wanted to be successful.

Rich Campe

Rich graduated as a Certified Coach with Tony Robbins in 1991, and he is currently part of the Jim Rohn International Coaching team. Although Rich is a very successful business owner and entrepreneur, his real passion lies in helping people reach their true potential. Rich's clients include Bank of America, Northwestern Mutual, AXA, Ameriprise, and Planco, to name a few. Rich resides in Charlotte, NC, with his lovely wife, Catherine, and their two children, Camden and Lawson. For more information, visit his website at www.richcampe.com. To contact Rich, send an email to info@richcampe.com or telephone 704-752-7760.

Chapter Six

THINKING ABOUT THINKING
Start in the Beginning... Start with Thinking

Rich Campe

A ccording to one of Harvard's Top 10 articles from the last century, *"Managing Oneself,"* written by the late Peter F. Drucker:

"Success in the knowledge economy comes to those who know themselves – their strengths, their values and how they best perform. History's Great Achiever's – A Napoleon, a daVinci, a Mozart – have always managed themselves. That, in large measure, is what makes them great achievers. But they are rare exceptions, so unusual both in their talents and their accomplishments as to be considered outside the boundaries of ordinary human existence. Now, most of us, even those of us with modest endowments, will have to learn to manage ourselves."

Do people really change or is it that people, having been diverted in life, simply remember who they once were or who they were really supposed to be? As a coach, I have often pondered this question, introspectively and with colleagues, clients, friends and family.

Oddly enough, after years of asking this question, the answer is ultimately "NO," we do not change at the core of our being and with regard to our dominant-thinking tendencies. This is actually good news because it means we're not all the same, and by appreciating the value of diversity and complimenting one another, our lives are enriched exponentially. Yet, we find so few people celebrating themselves and so many desiring to be something they are not. Sure, we can temporarily adapt; but, like swimming upstream, we can only do it for short periods of time. As coaches, we can waste a lot of time and money helping our clients become someone they're not while the client is doing the same thing. We experience a much greater return on our time, energy and passion when we seek to understand our God-given gifts and fully develop and leverage them.

Let me illustrate this point through a true story. In the early 1980's, my associate, mentor and friend, Jack Wilder, was asked by the CEO of Sharper Image to be a guest speaker on a panel with **Michael Jordan** and **Walter Payton** with the intent to provide leadership to the inner-city school kids from the heart of Chicago, IL. Mr. Payton and Mr. Jordan both explained the importance of working hard, being disciplined and staying focused in order to fulfill their dream of being whatever they wanted to be in life.

The CEO asked Jack, "Jack, you don't look like you believe what Mr. Jordan and Mr. Payton are saying?" Jack's reply was… "I do believe what they are saying is important; however, it's not the most important." For example, "Even though I'm 6'6," I could spend every waking hour doing every drill that Mr. Jordan does every day and still never become the center for an NBA basketball team due to my genetics. Mr. Jordan has taken his God-given gifts and developed them."

I believe we must first start with who we are and then work to develop from this core. What about becoming an agent, trainer, coach, doctor and so many other careers? So many people waste precious time trying to be something they will never become. Just because we work hard does not mean we will succeed. The reality is, we can work hard, be disciplined and stay focused while looking for a sunrise in the west and it's not going to happen. We must start with the core person and coach them to be more of who they already are and not make someone into someone we think they are or can become.

The late Dr. Robert S. Hartman (1910-1973) was the author of more than ten books, over 100 articles, and the translator of six books. His life-long quest was to answer the question, "What is good?" - and to answer the question in such a way that good could be organized to help preserve and enhance the value of human life. Dr. Hartman, whose work in the area of thinking earned him the coveted nomination for the Noble Peace Prize, developed a way to measure and track thinking. This incredible discovery allows us to very quickly understand who we really are at the core and, more importantly, measure our progress in becoming the best version of ourselves. In Dr. Hartman's work in the science of Formal Axiology, he was able to boil down all thinking into three primary dimensions. Much like all color is derived from the three primary colors, all thinking is derived from three primary dimensions. Dr. Hartman called these three dimensions of thinking Intrinsic (how we relate with self and others), Extrinsic (what we do and the roles we play), and Systemic (the rules we apply towards the world and ourselves). He further divided these three thinking dimensions into two categories, the internal and external worlds. Externally, it's how we think and view the world around us from these three dimensions. Internally, it's how we think about and perceive ourselves from these three dimensions. Altogether, this gives us six thinking dimensions to measure.

With this basic understanding of what these dimensions represent, we can then measure our thinking capacity or clarity in each particular area and whether we're attentive to or disregarding each thinking dimension. The first measurement represents our thinking strengths and weaknesses, while the second represents our thinking biases. By combining the dimensions, we can gain an even deeper understanding of a person. To help you understand, here's some additional explanation of the terms:

1. Clarity is like the aperture, hole or opening through which light is admitted on a camera. A larger hole lets more light in which exposes more on film, with the opposite being true as well. It represents how much we see within each dimension of thinking.

2. Bias represents whether we're paying attention to this dimension of our thinking or not and the degree to

which our behaviors are determined by this dimension. The question is, are we over or under emphasizing this area of our thinking?

3. The combination of bias patterns and clarities across all six dimensions represent our thinking DNA and who we are at our core.

In summary, no matter how great the business plans, strategies, tools, seminars, books and coaching, we will only reach our fullest impact potential when we start with who we are at the core. Start in the beginning... start with thinking!

Here are three easy steps to write in your journal to discover who you are and who you are meant to be.

1. *Take the Scientific MindScan and review it with a highlighter and pen.*
2. *Expose your MindScan and yourself to a few people you trust and respect to get valuable feedback.*
3. *Work with a coach to assist you in reading the MindScan and unfolding the greatness within yourself.*

We MUST learn to Maximize our Strengths and Manage our potential Weaknesses!

To receive a free sample MindScan of one of your natural strengths, go to:

www.richcampe.com/powerofcoaching
User ID: powerofcoaching   Password: success

Mark Rooney

Mark Rooney, CLU, ChFC, CFO, started his career in Los Angeles, CA, in 1973. He has spent all 33 years with AXA Equitable, holding many different positions including President of the Variable Life Company, Chairman of the Trust Company and of the Brokerage Company, President of four different Regions and Divisions and Chief Marketing Officer. He currently leads the AXA office in Los Angeles with over 200 advisors and nearly 25 million in base commissions and fees. To reach Mark at AXA Advisors, LLC Los Angeles Marketing Center, telephone 310-231-7770.

Chapter Seven

BUSINESS PLANS REQUIRE BUSY-NESS

Mark Rooney

T o be successful in BUSINESS, you must be successful in BUSY-NESS. It has been said that successful people have: Places to go. People to see. Things to do...**BUT,** how do you get these places, people, and things? How do you effectively structure your "BUSY-NESS" to optimize your success?

Coaches call the answer to these questions a **GAME PLAN.** In our world, we tend to call it a **BUSINESS PLAN.** Many of the most successful coaches are so committed to this planning process that not only do they have a strategy for each game, but actually script the first 15 or 20 plays.

This method of taking your plan from the overall goal to the most specific details can be very meaningful to our work in the financial services industry.

We have adopted a 5-step (5-page) program that has proven very effective over the years. A big percentage of the purpose for a written business plan is to force you to think through how you will achieve what you want. The rest of the reason for the written plan is as a communications tool for those who will participate in or coach you through execution of what you say you will do.

Step (Page) 1 of the plan is establishing goals. The primary goal of any business is to have a profit, thus these goals relate to income. The plan will carry out for five years, but the first few are the most important and will involve several components.

> **Budget** – The Small Business Administration (SBA) says the major reason for the failure of new business endeavors is undercapitalization. Make sure your income (revenue-expenses) projections are large enough to cover your lifestyle expenditures.

> **Revenue** – This is the total earnings anticipated each year from fees, commissions, trails, bonuses, renewals, etc. Most new business owners believe they will double their revenues in year two (and many do) but use a more moderate growth rate. 20% is realistic in your early years.

> **Expenses** – They should not be high in your early years and will probably relate to transportation, technology, marketing, training and Errors & Omission Insurance. You might estimate 15% to 20% of your total revenue.

> **Profit** – This is really what is left when you subtract your expenses from total revenues. Make sure the outcome is larger than your necessary budget (or

that you have resources to cover the difference) and that you save/invest the remainder wisely.

You are in the financial advisory business, and you want to make sure that *"the shoemaker's kids have nice shoes."*

Step (Page) 2 – Convert goal to task. What is it going to take to make Step 1 a reality? This will, of course, vary by the type of practice you are developing, but your firm should have some good statistics to guide you. The purpose of this step is to **focus** you on the type and volume of **activities** that will be necessary to reach your goal.

An example follows. You can adjust the numbers to your situation:

Anticipated Earnings	$120,000
Average Earnings per "Sale"	$1,200
Number of Projected Sales Necessary	100
Convert to Weekly Number	2
Closing Interviews to Make 2 "Sales"	4
Opening Interviews Set 4 Closings	8

Assuming a 20% fall off/charge rate, if you set **10** opening interviews a week and the rest hold true, you will be on track. Now you can focus on getting 10 interviews per week, and the rest should fall into place. But how do you do this? That is **Step 3**.

Step (Page) 3 – Determining the markets and methods you will use to get the 10 interviews set. Some tips:

Markets are people (not products, industries, or geography). Make sure they are the type of people you want to work with that have a need for what you do. The more homogeneous they are by geography, profession, interests, etc., the quicker your primary interview setting methods will be by referral, Center of Influence or networks.

Choose multiple markets – you don't want a tax law change, local industry downturn, legislative adjustment or something else beyond your control, critically impairing a business you have worked hard to build. Also, it is less daunting to set two or three interviews in each of three or four markets than it is to get ten in one.

Use one more of the eight methods possible to acquire an interview:

- Referrals
- Center of Influence
- Networks
- Mail (electronic or not)
- Advertising (electronic or not)
- Seminars/Trade Shows
- Face to Face
- Telephone (warm or cold)

Choose as many as you need to get the necessary interviews in each market.

Quantify the contract ratios and time commitment to market development (prospecting) in each market. Referrals may have a 3 to 1 ratio. Therefore, you could reasonably make six calls to get two appointments and spend an hour or less. Cold calls may have a 12 to 1 ratio and take 25 calls for appointments. This may be two to three hours.

Step (Page) 4 – Time Management. Most new business people will argue they work 50 to 60 hours per week or more. Can you get all you need to get done in that amount of time? YES!!

Alec Mackenzie, often called the Father of Time Management, spoke of the importance in any endeavor of seeking the "essence" (most important) activities for success. He then gave thought to the "Pareto Principle" or "80-20 Rule." He recommended spending 80% on "essence" activity and 20% on all else.

In a sales-oriented business, much of your success is based on your persuasive ability, and the only thing you can persuade is people. You need to persuade people to see you (prospecting) and persuade them to do business with you ("selling" them on an idea, a product, a concept, etc.).

The closer your days could be spent to 80% with people, either prospecting or interviews, the better. But, there is also more to do that might look like this:

Hours to Prospecting – **10**. Take this number directly from the markets, methods, ratios and time commitments you established in Step Three.

Hours to Closing Interviews – **5** at 1 hour or so. Some longer, some shorter.

Hours to Opening Interviews – **10**. Your number of interview hours will come from your work in Step 2.

Hours to Meetings – **3**, depending on your firm.

Hours to Class – **5**, again based on your firm's training schedule.

Hours to Study – **5**, ditto above.

Hours to Correspondence on Client Service – **3**. This will grow over time, but study and class will diminish.

Hours to Case Preparation – **5**. Try to do this in predictable, non "client visitation" hours.

This totals 46. Well below the 50 or 60 predicted, leaving plenty of time for "miscellaneous."

Step (Page) 5 – The ideal schedule!! Take all the activities from Step 4 and place them on a weekly calendar as to what you will do when. The more you can target and hold to your market development and interviewing times, as well as all else, the more "you will control your business rather than it control you."

Yes, this is idealistic in a "human nature" business where things can change, but without some planned schedule, all you have is anarchy and confusion.

Envision 15 "cells." Morning, afternoon, and evening, 5 days a week (maybe leave out Friday evening and add Saturday morning). Try to fill each cell with the type and number of activities you decided upon in Steps 2, 3 and 4.

We think of a week beginning with an empty sheet as our single greatest enemy. It can be quite psychologically defeating in a business that feeds heavily off of positive attitude.

A full and well thought-out schedule walking into the week can be your single greatest ally.

Conclusion:

When a person is new in their career or even at the beginning of a new year or planning cycle, thinking through (and putting in writing) the places you will go, the people you will see and the things you will do, is going to lead almost anyone to a more certain level of achievement.

Structuring your BUSY-NESS will improve your business.

The five steps of generic planning will help.

One other opportunity a good plan provides, especially when you are new, is that you can **consciously** build new habit patterns that will service you well far into the future.

Farmers love clean, fertile fields, for if you plant and nurture well, you will reap the crop you hope for. They hate "weedy" fields as, before you can start, you have to clean off the field. This literally makes it twice as hard to achieve the same outcome. When a person is new, or even when they are prepared to change, seeking a better result, the field ideas, habits and procedures properly planted and nurtured, will grow well.

Unfortunately (or fortunately), what we have reviewed in this chapter does not come naturally to most. It requires a significant amount of guidance, coaching, reinforcement and management. Fortunate is the associate who has a manager or some other coach, who can work them through the planning process. The more compelling the strategy leading to the greatest level of detailed activity (like the game plan and 15 scripted plays), the greater predictability of success. Ongoing monitoring and adjustment of the plan will be the most meaningful and constructive "performance review" a manager could ever do.

The highest cost of entry into our business is the opportunity cost (I could have spent my time doing this or something else). Properly constructed, a good plan should give comfort that, executed to, the person will be farther ahead five years from now in this endeavor than any alternative.

In an era when enough productivity to achieve necessary retention and development goals is virtually a necessity for survival, can anyone in a leadership role afford not to take advantage of such a powerful coaching tool and opportunity?

You can download Mark's five page Word.doc template version of this plan by going to:

www.ThePowerOfCoaching.com.

John Assaraf

John Assaraf is a best-selling author, speaker, and entrepreneur. His expertise in helping organizations and individuals achieve success has landed him on ABC, CBS and NBC television worldwide. John recently made his cameo appearance in the new hit movie *The Secret*, which can be viewed at www.onecoach.com/secret. In the last 20 years, he has built four multi-million dollar companies, including growing RE/MAX of Indiana to over 1500 sales associates. John is now the Founder of OneCoach, a company committed to helping entrepreneurs and professionals achieve financial freedom and live extraordinary lives. For more information, visit www.onecoach.com.

Chapter Eight

THE POWER OF HAVING A VISION

HOW QUANTUM PHYSICS, YOUR BRAIN, AND YOUR HEART MANIFEST YOUR VISION AND GOALS

John Assaraf

F or many years, I heard that you had to start with a vision for your business or your life if you really wanted to succeed, but no one could explain to me why it was needed or how it worked from a practical or scientific standpoint.

When I was young and naïve, I was skeptical and wanted empirical evidence showing me why I should invest my thoughts and time into really thinking about a vision for my life and business, and why getting absolutely clear by writing it down was imperative to my achieving success.

Even though I couldn't find adequate answers at the time, reluctantly, I did as others suggested purely because they were far more successful than I. As I was told "don't ask so many questions" and "just do it," I temporarily gave up my need for so many answers— but not for long.

At the ripe young age of 21, I created a grand vision for my life and my career. Even though I had only graduated from high school, and everyone told me that "you need a college degree to really succeed," I took a different approach and got into business at a very young age. For the next 26 years, I stayed on a healthy mental diet to train my brain and followed the belief of allowing the universe to guide me and bring me whatever I needed to fulfill my visions of being financially free and living an extraordinary life.

After building four multi-million dollar businesses— one of which grosses more than $5 billion a year in sales—and having made millions of dollars for myself and others, I began to search for the answers to the question I'd had 25 years earlier—"Why is having a clear and precise vision so important?" I couldn't help wanting to know why. As a child I was very curious, and my parents could not answer many of the questions I had about success. After all, they only had a total of 5 years of school between them and had never made more than $30 thousand in a year.

Since I wanted more for myself, I sought out the best minds, researchers, and teachers in the world to teach me how to have an abundant life in all areas. So, what did I learn that you can apply immediately to benefit from my lessons? Simple: Without a clear and precise vision of exactly what it is you want, you'll never reach it or have it.

Now, of course, I will not leave you hanging without understanding why.

My research has taken me into the world of quantum physics and neuroscience for the answer to the question, "Why is it so important to start with a vision?"

Let's start with the world of quantum physics. First and foremost, quantum physics is the study of how the very small world, one we cannot see with our eyes, operates. Since we live in two worlds—one that we can see—and one that we cannot, it's important for us to know what these two worlds offer us. Scientifically, we now know that even though we cannot see any connection, both worlds are totally interconnected at every level.

Newtonian physics helps us understand how to navigate the known physical world, and quantum physics helps us to understand the very intelligent non-physical world in which everything is connected to everything else and from which all known physical "things" are manifested.

What we've discovered in this new realm of quantum research is that whatever we focus on and emotionalize often, is what we will attract and actually see in the quantum field of all possibilities, or better yet, probabilities.

As weird as this may sound, this is now being proven without a shadow of a doubt. What this means is, the more clearly focused we are on exactly what we want, the easier and faster we'll manifest everything we need to make it a physical reality.

Since all material things move from the non-physical to the physical reality, our vision and goals are paramount in the process of achievement. Our vision and focus acts like a magnet that attracts and connects the pieces together.

Another thing to keep in mind is that the universe operates by natural laws, exact precision, and perfect order. Our vision, then, must also be precise and exact in our mind in order for whatever we need to be attracted and shown to us by the intelligent forces that govern all of creation. When we focus our brain on what we want, we actually increase the amplitude of the cellular vibration and cause the "attraction" factor to really take shape.

Just like a magnifying glass can focus the sun's rays and create a fire, focusing on our vision and goals keeps you in the right vibration and attraction field.

When we choose a vision or goal that is bigger than our current reality, we are in essence creating a gap or a vacuum between what we want and where we currently are. We know from natural law that nature fills a void or gap in the fastest and most efficient ways possible.

Now for the "brain and heart" part of the equation.

The latest research proves that when we're fully engaged and emotionalized in our clear vision, we emit a frequency from our brain and heart that penetrates and permeates all space and time, bringing forth to us everything that's in resonance with the image we're holding. The frequency we emit is our personal electromagnetic frequency. Just like a radio station that sends out a signal, we send ours out based on our dominating thoughts at a conscious and subconscious level.

Just imagine the way an apple seed attracts the nutrients it needs from the soil to grow its roots, and then, once it sprouts above the ground, the sun adds its magic and food through photosynthesis. Then, lo and behold….the seed becomes an apple tree.

You, too, will attract exactly what you need to realize your dreams when you really start to believe and feel your vision becoming a reality. It's the clear and consistent vibration of your vision that brings forth your needs. You provide the seed, the universe provides the resources.

Therefore, you must now make your "new vision" inside your brain more real than the current results in your outside world. Then, and only then, will the universe begin to present its riches to you in the most convenient and efficient ways possible.

Your clear vision is your seed. Choose it wisely and precisely, and riches beyond your imagination in every area of your life shall be yours.

John Assaraf
Founder, One Coach
www.onecoach.com

Phillip C. Richards

 Phillip C. Richards, CFP, CLU, RHU is the Chairman of the Board and CEO of the affiliated companies under North Star Resource Group. Phil has been a featured speaker in over a dozen countries on topics ranging from strategic planning and leadership to alternate distribution systems in the financial services industry. Phil co-chairs the Industry's "Task Force for The Future" and serves on the Board of Directors for the American College Endowment Foundation, the LIFE Foundation, the North Star Charitable Foundation, and the Arizona Heart Foundation. Phil is the author of The 25 Secrets to Sustainable Success. Visit NorthStarFinancial.com for information.

Chapter Nine

USING QUARTERLY REVIEWS TO COACH

Phillip C. Richards

Q uarterly reviews serve as a great tool in coaching advisors. Because of the unstructured nature of the advisor's role, accountability is, in most cases, essential, especially in the early years.

The quarterly review is something that any publicly traded company in America is very familiar with because every 90 days or so, they are held accountable by the Wall Street analysts who evaluate their performance. If this process is effective for CEOs of huge, publicly traded corporations, why should it be anything less for our advisors, in terms of helping them set and reach their goals?

Conducting Quarterly Reviews

We begin the process by scheduling quarterly reviews for every half hour, allowing a 20-minute time slot for each advisor. We turn our cell phones and computers off during the reviews, of course.

There may be one or two personal icebreaking questions at the beginning of a quarterly-review.

The Quarterly-Review Questionnaire

We use a structured form during each advisor's quarterly review. This questionnaire addresses our advisors' annual goals in many areas—professional designations, life commissions, and company and firm credits. Advisors could also be striving for individual awards. So, the starting point is to look at the individual bogeys, targets, and goals recorded in each advisor's annual plan.

At the top of the typical quarterly-review questionnaire is the advisor's name, review date, and the year they started in the business. This gives us perspective about where their progress should be at any given point in time. When you're dealing with many advisors, it's not easy to remember the year each started in business. As you grow your firm, systems like this can spare you some of the pain that we have experienced.

Your Key Goal

One of the questions at the top of the sheet is, "What is your key goal this year?" They may have 20 goals, but we focus on the one key goal that, if achieved, would automatically make their year a success.

It is always a quantitative goal, but it may not have a quantitative name. For example, Million Dollar Round Table doesn't have a quantitative name, but the goal is quantitative because the requirement changes annually, and in any given year, advisors know the exact amount of first-year commissions they need to qualify. I like to point out, if you can measure it, you can manage it. If you can't measure it, you can't manage it.

Your Critical Number

The second question is, "What is your critical number?" That number will be different for each advisor. The critical number is that one number you fight for and have confidence in, and if you attain it, your other goals are likely to fall into place.

The critical number is not the same as the annual goal. Annual MDRT qualification cannot be a critical number because a critical number must be much shorter in duration—usually daily, and later, weekly. The most common critical number for our advisors, especially new ones, is to always have 30 appointments with prospective clients written in their appointment books. This number for new advisors lets everyone know whether they have won or lost today!

Expose the Insanity of Wishful Thinking

The next two questions are about the advisor's key annual goal: "Are you ahead, or are you behind?" and "By how much?" We want to quantify where they are and what they need to do. If an advisor is significantly behind in his progress toward his annual goal, then we reach a critical part of the interview, asking, "Do you want to adjust (lower) your goal?" Most advisors will say no, necessitating the next question, "What activity are you going to change to alter the result you've been getting?" In other words, he either has to change his goal or change his activity level.

So far, we've looked at the goal from an annual perspective. Next, we transition to a quarterly time frame, asking, "What did you say you would do in the last 90 days; and what, in fact, have you done during that period?" There will be one of two outcomes—either the advisor has done what he said he would, or he has not done what he said he would. If he missed his quarterly goal, the next question is "Why?"

We try to get advisors to look candidly and honestly at their performance, measure it and think critically about it. When we don't achieve our goals, its human nature to try not to think about it, to look for a foxhole, or go into denial. The objective is to bring the actual data into the open and light up the foxhole.

If an advisor doesn't hit his quarterly goal, chances are that he's behind on his annual goal, too. In this case, we're right back where we started—we either have to lower the annual goal, or the advisor must commit to a different activity level than the one which didn't meet his recent goal.

Sometimes, the choice is clear. For example, an advisor whose goal was $100,000 of first-year commissions could lower that goal without any repercussions. But, if an advisor's goal is to qualify for MDRT, he cannot lower his goal. He must raise his activity level to meet the goal because advisors in their fifth year or beyond must qualify for Million Dollar Round Table to remain internal with our organization.

What's Your Why

The next question is, "What is your motivation to hit your goal?" Our axiom is, "If you have a big enough *why*, you will figure out the *what* and the *how*." That's what we're trying to get at when we ask, "What is your motivation? What gets you out of bed in the morning and off to work to achieve something?" Advisors have a passion for the "why" that will motivate them to hit their goals. It could be, "I want to lead the organization," or "I want to buy my parents a home." If they have a big enough why, then they'll figure out how to do it.

Personal Income

Next, we shift to income. This is a gut check question: "What was your income last year?" The next question is critical: "Were you satisfied with that income?" If they say yes, that's great; however, that's not the normal response. The normal response is, "No, I'm not satisfied with it." Why is that the typical answer? Because advisors are hunters, not gatherers. They eat what they kill, and thank God for that. It wouldn't matter, quantitatively, what their income was—they seldom find complete contentment in it. They're striving to be better and achieve more at all times. That's what makes them great advisors. They love goals and continue to increase them. They convert dreams to goals by giving them deadlines. Field leaders should strive to be the catalyst in this process.

Income is in the advisor's control, so we ask, "What do you want your income to be this year?" The next question is even more important: "Why do you want that amount of income?" Again, we're getting to the advisor's motivation to hit his personal goal.

Life Production

Next, we review the advisor's life production goal for last year and ask, "What will it be this year?" Because our firm is a life-based, financial-planning organization, we believe that the person who controls the life insurance sale controls the relationship.

Then, we ask our advisors if they are ahead or behind on their life production goal and by how much. We drill down again on this goal to see where they are on an annual basis.

The final question about income is, "What are you going to do differently to increase your income to a level where you will be satisfied?" We want to end this part of the discussion talking about activity: "What are you going to do to improve your results?"

It has been said that things that do not change remain the same. To change their results, advisors must change their activity. Assuming that our advisors keep good records, we then work with them to review their activity over the last month, quarter, and year and make the necessary upward adjustments.

Michael E. Gerber revisited this concept in *The E Myth Revisited*. He calls it "information systems" and lists the following benchmarks:

- How many calls were made?
- How many prospects were reached?
- How many appointments were scheduled?
- How many appointments were confirmed?
- How many appointments were held?
- How many needs-analysis presentations were scheduled, confirmed, and completed?
- How many solutions presentations were scheduled, confirmed, and completed?
- What was the average dollar amount?

Gerber says that this exercise will tell you which of your advisors are using your selling system and which are not. It will tell you what needs to be changed.[1]

Lifelong Learning

From there, the quarterly review moves to, "What tests have you taken and passed in the last 90 days?" We're talking about professional designations. From an educational point of view, we're interested in what progress they're making on their CLU and ChFC, and once they have those designations, their CFP. This is a profession, and the litmus test of one's devotion to it is their commitment to obtaining these designations. Our clients deserve nothing less.

---

[1] Michael E. Gerber, *The E Myth Revisited: Why Most Small Businesses Don't Work and What to Do About It*, 1995 and 2001, HarperCollins Publishers, New York, pp. 247–248.

From a professional point of view, we would like our people to have all of these designations. We want people who are committed to a lifetime of learning, and there are ample opportunities available in our industry for people to do that. No one could learn all of the information available on financial planning in one lifetime. There's just too much information to master, and it's growing exponentially. And let's not forget that people want specialists, not generalists, in this complex environment that we live and work.

Contests, Challenges, and Solutions

After the educational piece, we come back to company and firm contests. We ask, "Where are you in terms of those milestones?"

Then, we ask them to name the three greatest challenges in their business, regardless of their order. We write them down and say, "Let's take each one of them, and tell me what you're going to do about it." We love to have advisors verbalize their answers and hear them talk out loud about themselves. It gives us some special insight into the inner-person we're coaching.

From there, we go to a series of three questions and three possible solutions. This section of the quarterly review is focused on helping the advisor grow as an individual.

The three questions are: "What goals are you putting off?"; "What will you have accomplished before the end of the next quarter?"; and "What is your plan to increase administrative and marketing support?" We should continuously try to convince advisors to delegate $10- and $20-an-hour work so that they focus on the $500-an-hour work—namely, being in front of people. We want to keep the planes in the air, not on the tarmac.

Finally, we ask our advisors how North Star can help them achieve their goals, how they want us to hold them accountable so they can meet their goals, and what the firm is or is not doing that can help them. We sometimes ask newer advisors, "If you were CEO of this firm, what would you do, stop doing, or do differently?" Fresh ideas provide us with new building stones.

As you can see, our quarterly reviews reveal in-depth insight into each advisor's mindset, motivation, and progress. These reviews provide a systematic way for managers to hold advisors accountable for their performance and keep them on track toward their goals. It also ensures that we connect with them regularly and find out what's going on in their professional and personal lives.

Your Turn to Coach

⇒ **Hold Your Advisors Accountable**—Review critical performance data for your advisors on a quarterly basis. This allows you to hold them accountable for their performance, help them stay on track to meet their goals, and build your professional relationship with them.

⇒ **Discover the Big "Why"**—Understand each advisor's passion and commitment to his or her goals.

⇒ **Require Results**—Advisors who are not on track to meet their goal must lower that goal or increase their activity to get back on track.

⇒ **Exchange Deliverables**—Require minimum production levels in return for the value that your firm delivers to your advisors that makes your value proposition unique.

⇒ **Teach Advisors that Activity Solves All Problems**—Al Granum's One Card System is timeless and applies to experienced as well as new advisors.

⇒ **Use Professional Designations as Proof of Commitment**—Advisors and leaders in our profession should offer our clients nothing less than professionalism and a commitment to lifelong learning.

⇒ **"What You Cannot Avoid, Welcome"**—As this Chinese proverb suggests, change is inevitable, and growth is our choice. Coach your advisors to get out of their comfort zones and into growth opportunities.

WHO AM I?
Author Unknown

You may know me...I'm your constant companion.
I'm your greatest helper.
I'm your heaviest burden.
I will push you onward...or drag you down to failure.

I am at your command if you choose to use me.
Half the tasks you do...can be turned over to me.
I'm able to do them quickly and I'm able to do them
the same every time.

I'm easily managed - all you have to do is be firm with me.
Show me exactly how you want it done.
After a few lessons, I'll do it automatically.

I am the servant of all great men and women.
And of course, the servant of all the failures as well.
I've made all the great individuals who have ever been great,
And all the losers, too.

I work with the precision of a computer
and the intelligence of a human being.
You may run me for profit, or you may run me to ruin...
it makes no difference to me.

Take me. Be easy with me and I will destroy you.
Be firm with me and I'll put the world at your feet.

Who am I?

I am your Habit.

www.ThePowerOfCoaching.com

Jim Rohn

 The following article was submitted by Jim Rohn, America's Foremost Business Philosopher. To subscribe to the Free Jim Rohn Weekly E-Zine, go to www.jimrohn.com or send a blank email to subscribe@jimrohn.com. Copyright © 2005 Jim Rohn International. All rights reserved worldwide.

Chapter Ten

THE FORMULA FOR FAILURE AND SUCCESS

Jim Rohn

F ailure is not a single, cataclysmic event. We do not
fail overnight. Failure is the inevitable result of an
accumulation of poor thinking and poor choices. To put
it more simply, failure is nothing more than a few
errors in judgment repeated every day.

Now, why would someone make an error in judgment
and then be so foolish as to repeat it every day? The
answer is because he or she does not think that it
matters.

On their own, our daily acts do not seem that
important. A minor oversight, a poor decision, or a
wasted hour generally doesn't result in an instant and
measurable impact. More often than not, we escape
from any immediate consequences of our deeds.

If we have not bothered to read a single book in the past
ninety days, this lack of discipline does not seem to
have any immediate impact on our lives. And since
nothing drastic happened to us after the first ninety
days, we repeat this error in judgment for another
ninety days, and on and on it goes. Why? Because it

doesn't seem to matter. And herein lies the great danger. Far worse than not reading the books is not even realizing that it matters!

Those who eat too many of the wrong foods are contributing to a future health problem, but the joy of the moment overshadows the consequence of the future. It does not seem to matter. Those who smoke too much or drink too much go on making these poor choices year after year after year... because it doesn't seem to matter. But the pain and regret of these errors in judgment have only been delayed for a future time. Consequences are seldom instant; instead, they accumulate until the inevitable day of reckoning finally arrives and the price must be paid for our poor choices - choices that didn't seem to matter.

Failure's most dangerous attribute is its subtlety. In the short term those little errors don't seem to make any difference. We do not seem to be failing. In fact, sometimes these accumulated errors in judgment occur throughout a period of great joy and prosperity in our lives. Since nothing terrible happens to us, since there are no instant consequences to capture our attention, we simply drift from one day to the next, repeating the errors, thinking the wrong thoughts, listening to the wrong voices and making the wrong choices. The sky did not fall in on us yesterday; therefore, the act was probably harmless. Since it seemed to have no measurable consequence, it is probably safe to repeat. But we must become better educated than that!

If at the end of the day when we made our first error in judgment the sky had fallen in on us, we undoubtedly would have taken immediate steps to ensure that the act would never be repeated again. Like the child who places his hand on a hot burner despite his parents' warnings, we would have had an instantaneous experience accompanying our error in judgment.

Unfortunately, failure does not shout out its warnings as our parents once did. This is why it is imperative to refine our philosophy in order to be able to make better choices. With a powerful, personal philosophy guiding our every step, we become more aware of our errors in judgment and more aware that each error really does matter.

Now, here is the great news. Just like the formula for failure, the formula for success is easy to follow: It's a few simple disciplines practiced every day.

Now, here is an interesting question worth pondering: How can we change the errors in the formula for failure into the disciplines required in the formula for success? The answer is by making the future an important part of our current philosophy.

Both success and failure involve future consequences, namely the inevitable rewards or unavoidable regrets resulting from past activities. If this is true, why don't more people take time to ponder the future? The answer is simple: They are so caught up in the current moment that it doesn't seem to matter. The problems and the rewards of today are so absorbing to some human beings that they never pause long enough to think about tomorrow.

But what if we did develop a new discipline to take just a few minutes every day to look a little further down the road? We would then be able to foresee the impending consequences of our current conduct. Armed with that valuable information, we would be able to take the necessary action to change our errors into new success-oriented disciplines. In other words, by disciplining ourselves to see the future in advance, we would be able to change our thinking, amend our errors and develop new habits to replace the old.

One of the exciting things about the formula for success - a few simple disciplines practiced every day - is that the results are almost immediate. As we voluntarily change daily errors into daily disciplines, we experience positive results in a very short period of time. When we change our diet, our health improves noticeably in just a few weeks. When we start exercising, we feel a new vitality almost immediately. When we begin reading, we experience a growing awareness and a new level of self-confidence. Whatever new discipline we begin to practice daily will produce exciting results that will drive us to become even better at developing new disciplines.

The real magic of new disciplines is that they will cause us to amend our thinking. If we were to start today to read the books, keep a journal, attend the classes, listen more and observe more, then today would be the first day of a new life leading to a better future. If we were to start today to try harder, and in every way make a conscious and consistent effort to change subtle and deadly errors into constructive and rewarding disciplines, we would never again settle for a life of existence - not once we have tasted the fruits of a life of substance!

To Your Success,

Jim Rohn

This article was submitted by Jim Rohn, America's Foremost Business Philosopher. To subscribe to the Free Jim Rohn Weekly E-zine, go to www.jimrohn.com or send a blank email to subscribe@jimrohn.com. Copyright© 2005 Jim Rohn International. All rights reserved worldwide.

Jon Berghoff

 Jon Berghoff, co-founder of Global Empowerment Coaching, has spoken to well over 20,000 entrepreneurs, business owners, sales professionals, and managers. Starting at age 17, Jon has achieved numerous top sales awards in various industries. As a manager for an upscale health club, he developed a strategy to sell to corporations and took a club with no sales team and brought it to be one of the most profitable health clubs in the United States. Jon is available to speak on management, leadership, sales training, self motivation, and personal development topics. To have Jon as a speaker, coach, or trainer, please visit his website at www.globalempowermentcoaching.com.

Chapter Eleven

MASTER SELF MANAGEMENT

Jon Berghoff

I 've had the great pleasure to instruct, inspire, and lead best-selling authors, the world's top financial planners, a world-class mountain climber, executive coaches, and literally thousands of other independent business owners, salespeople, and managers. The more I've learned about these people – and myself – the more I become aware of one profound underlying truth: We are all the same.

There is an innate presence within every business owner who wants to feel success. Sometimes the levels of desire, passion, and commitment may vary, but at a deep, core level of being, our common denominator is a wanting for fulfillment; and in the business arena, that means success. This fundamental truth always brings us abruptly to one key question.

How is it that some people get what they want and others do not? Many lives, long hours, and carefully spent resources have been invested, trying to find the answer to this timeless question. I'll give my best shot at answering it; but before reading on, I challenge you to embark on your own personal quest to find this answer. I have always found that the process of searching for answers is significantly more enlightening than just looking at the answers themselves.

I do not claim that my philosophies are the only answer to this question; however, I can say that I've found some fundamental truths that seem to match up when I look at all of the top achieving individuals I've worked with. In case you cannot read any further, your kids are yelling at you, your wife or husband is calling on the other line, or your new puppy is peeing on the carpet, here is my answer, wrapped up in a few words: The Art of Self Management.

Before I unveil some of the deepest, most enlightening secrets that I have discovered on how to master The Art of Self Management, you, the reader, have one prerequisite to meet; you must accept responsibility for implementing this information within your life and the lives of those who you lead. This is the qualifying belief that master Self Managers never struggle with. They accept responsibility for everything.

Hal Elrod, one of my best friends, my business partner, and a best-selling author, always told me, "The moment I accept responsibility for *everything* in my life, is the moment I can create *anything* in my life." If you are ready to take responsibility, here are two of the key ingredients to The Art of Self Management.

I have rarely met an audience where the majority did not agree that they wished they had more time in their day. Coincidentally, I've always paid close attention to the top achievers of an organization and noticed during my surveys that they often do not express a desire for more time. They already understand the importance of what I call *Time Awareness*, the first ingredient for mastering The Art of Self Management.

Great Self Managers have all taught me that there are two requirements to developing a Time Awareness. Number one is to be honest with ourselves. Countless studies have been done where salespeople are asked how much time they think they are actually spending in front of customers. Every study, experiment, and report has shown that the average salesperson was only spending about half as much time in front of customers as they thought they were.

How can this be possible? Are they delusional, drugged, or in denial? Maybe so, but I'll tell you why this is an epidemic that is actually quite natural and should be expected. Here comes the answer: Most independent business owners spend a lot of time thinking about actions that they should be taking. The problem is that when these people go to bed at the end of the day, their minds cannot distinguish between time spent *working* vs. time spent *thinking about working*. Honesty is a must.

The second key ingredient to Time Awareness is being *in command* of our time. Here are the two most prevalent common denominators that I have witnessed with those who have this coveted command. First and foremost, Master Self Managers avoid accommodating outside influences at the expense of their own achievement. Avoiding accommodation is counter intuitive for many, because it seems at first glance to be a self-centered focus – and it is. While it is a self-centered philosophy, avoiding accommodation is actually better for all parties involved. If we accommodate others instead of sticking to our own plans, we usually spend the time with others wishing we were back at work, resulting in a lack of mental presence when we should be enjoying somebody's company.

The Master Self Manager not only knows how and when to say no to others, but they take command of the situation by negotiating another time to be with or enjoy this other person. If we don't stick to our own plan, we will probably just follow the plans of others... and, trust me, all of the outside forces that pull us off track, our cell phones, emails, friends, and family members, are never intentionally pulling us off track. Poor self managers just allow it to happen, through accommodation.

Predetermining our actions is the next step to being in command of our time. Very early in my sales career, I made a distinction that was eye opening. A moment spent planning my future was worth significantly more than each moment spent actually executing the plan. I soon realized that the *more* time I spent planning, the *better* I was at using my time well. Additionally, I noticed that the further into the future I planned, the more clarity I had on what was really important to do right now. Both of these factors gave me a confidence and conviction in my use of time that created dramatic results. The powerful combination of avoiding accommodation and predetermining our time will create immediate command of our time if we choose to implement these philosophies.

To accompany Time Awareness, there is fundamental quality that all Self Managers develop, and often can't explain exactly how they do it. This is what I would call Emotional Awareness. Almost any business owner, salesperson, and sales manager will readily admit that they have challenges, frustrations, fears, and setbacks to deal with on a regular basis. With that being said, I'm always curious why these same people rarely have a predetermined, executable, thought-out plan to manage their emotions during these inevitable tests of life.

Self Managers not only have a plan for managing their emotions, but they always have two qualities in common that allow for success in the process. Number one, they prepare themselves ahead of time for the challenges that they will face. This concept flies in the face of all the positive thinking, only attract what you want, happy-go-lucky strategies. As leaders – either of groups or of ourselves – we must be willing to accept challenges before they happen. The very first billionaire in the oil industry once said that there are only two steps to being successful, and one of them is to decide the price you are willing to pay to get there. That sounds a lot to me like accepting challenges before they happen.

After being honest about the challenges that will come, a master Self Manager has a very specific skill set which allows them to immediately turn a setback into a comeback, a challenge into an opportunity, a failure into a priceless lesson. This skill is what I call using the Meaning Muscle, and it is the key to Emotional Awareness.

The first book I ever read on personal development told me that my emotions were a product of my interpretations or the meaning I gave to the experience, never the experience.

A great example of this is: If you put two individuals on a roller coaster, who both give the same experience a different meaning, they will finish the ride with a totally different emotional (and physiological) response. One will be filled with fear, anxiety, and even terror. So much so, that the levels of adrenaline and insulin that are pumped into his body will cause the immune system to literally shut down. The other person will give the same experience a meaning of joy, ecstasy, and pleasure, resulting in endorphins and serotonin levels that are 40,000 times more potent than any heroin on the streets. Imagine that; same experience, different meaning, different emotions, and even different responses on a cellular level.

Here is my challenge for you. What are the roller coasters in your life? I guarantee there is somebody else in your industry who is riding the same ride, but giving it a different meaning. Because they are giving their roller coaster an empowering meaning (versus a disempowering one), they create more energy, more motivation, and more momentum. Consider this example during your next challenge, and ask yourself what are the opportunities that could come from making it through the experience?

For more information on The Art of Self Management, The Art of Sales Mastery, or The Art of Peak Performance, please contact Jon Berghoff at www.globalempowermentcoaching.com.

Brian Tracy

The following article was submitted by Brian Tracy, the most listened to audio author on personal and business success in the world today. He is the author/narrator of countless best-selling audio learning programs and the author of 16 books. All rights reserved worldwide. Copyright © 2006. Contact Brian Tracy at:

Brian Tracy International
462 Stevens Ave., Suite 202
Solana Beach, CA 92075
Phone: (858) 481-2977
www.BrianTracy.com

Chapter Twelve

LEADING AND MOTIVATING

Brian Tracy

I t's been said that "Leadership is not what you do, but who you are." This, however, is only partially true. Leadership is very much who you are, but it cannot be divorced from what you do. Who you are represents the inner person, and what you do represents the outer person. Each is dependent on the other for maximum effectiveness.

The starting point of motivational leadership is to begin seeing yourself as a role model, seeing yourself as an example to others. A key characteristic of leaders is that they set high standards of accountability for themselves and for their behaviors.

Motivational leadership is based on the Law of Indirect Effort. According to this law, most things in human life are achieved more easily by indirect means than they are by direct means. You more easily become a leader to others by demonstrating that you have the qualities of leadership than you do by ordering others to follow your directions.

In business, there are several kinds of power. Two of these are ascribed power and position power.

115

Position power is the power that comes with a job title or position in any organization. If you become a manager in a company, you automatically have certain powers and privileges that go along with your rank. You can order people about and make certain decisions. You can be a leader whether or not anyone likes you.

Ascribed power is the power you gain because of the kind of person you are. These are the men and women who are genuine leaders because of the quality of the people they have become, because of their characters and their personalities.

Perhaps the most powerful of motivational leaders is the person who practices what is called "servant leadership." Confucius said, "He who would be master must be servant of all." The person who sees himself or herself as a servant and who does everything possible to help others to perform at their best is practicing the highest form of servant leadership.

Over the years, we have been led to believe that leaders are those who stride boldly about, giving orders and making decisions for others to carry out. However, that is old school. Today's leader asks questions, listens carefully, plans diligently and then builds consensus among all those who are necessary for achieving the goals. The leader does not try to do it by himself or herself. The leader gets things done by helping others to do them.

This brings us to five of the qualities of motivational leaders. These are qualities that you already have to a certain degree and that you can develop further to stand out from the people around you in a very short period of time.

The first quality is *vision*. This is the one single quality that, more than anything, separates leaders from followers. Leaders have vision. Followers do not. Leaders have developed the ability to fix their eyes on the horizon and see greater possibilities. Followers are those whose eyes are fixed on the ground in front of them and who are so busy that they seldom look at themselves and their activities in a larger context. George Bernard Shaw summarized this quality of leaders; in the words of one of his characters: "Most men look at what is and ask, 'Why?' I instead look at what could be and ask, 'Why not?'"

The best way for you to motivate others is to be motivated yourself. The way to get others committed to achieving a goal or a result is to be totally committed yourself. The way to build loyalty to your organization, and to other people, is to be an example of loyalty in everything you say and do. These all are applications of the Law of Indirect Effort.

One requirement of leadership is the ability to choose an area of excellence. Just as a good general chooses the terrain on which to do battle, an excellent leader chooses the area in which he and others are going to do an outstanding job. The commitment to excellence is one of the most powerful of all motivators. All leaders who change people and organizations are enthusiastic about achieving excellence in a particular area.

The most motivational vision you can have for yourself and others is to "Be the best!" Many people don't yet realize that excellent performance in serving other people is an absolute, basic essential for survival in the economy of the future.

As a leader, your job is to be excellent at what you do, to be the best in your chosen field of endeavor. Your job is to have a vision of high standards in serving people. You not only exemplify excellence in your own behavior, but you also translate it to others so that they, too, become committed to this vision.

This is the key to servant leadership. It is the commitment to doing work of the highest quality in the service of other people, both inside and outside the organization. Leadership today requires an equal focus on the people who must do the job, on the one hand, and the people who are expected to benefit from the job, on the other.

The second quality, which is perhaps the single most respected quality of leaders, is *integrity*. Integrity is complete, unflinching honesty with regard to everything that you say and do. Integrity underlies all the other qualities. Your measure of integrity is determined by how honest you are in the critical areas of your life.

Integrity means: When someone asks you at the end of the day, "Did you do your very best?" you can look him in the eye and say, "Yes!" Integrity means: When someone asks you if you could have done it better, you can honestly say, "No, I did everything I possibly could."

Integrity means that you, as a leader, admit your shortcomings. It means that you work to develop your strengths and compensate for your weaknesses. Integrity means that you tell the truth, and that you live the truth in everything that you do and in all your relationships. Integrity means that you deal straightforwardly with people and situations and that you do not compromise what you believe to be true.

If the first two qualities of motivational leadership are vision and integrity, the third quality is the one that backs them both up. It is *courage*. It is the chief distinguishing characteristic of the true leader. It is almost always visible in the leader's words and actions. It is absolutely indispensable to success, happiness and the ability to motivate other people to be the best they can be.

In a way, it is easy to develop a big vision for yourself and for the person you want to be. It is easy to commit yourself to living with complete integrity. But it requires incredible courage to follow through on your vision and on your commitments. You see, as soon as you set a high goal or standard for yourself, you will run into all kinds of difficulties and setbacks.

Courage combined with integrity is the foundation of character. The first form of courage is your ability to stick to your principles, to stand for what you believe in and to refuse to budge unless you feel right about the alternative. Courage is also the ability to step out in faith and then to face the inevitable doubt and uncertainty that accompany every new venture.

The true leader has the courage to step away from the familiar and comfortable and to face the unknown with no guarantees of success. It is this ability to "boldly go where no man has gone before" that distinguishes you as a leader from the average person. This is the example that you must set if you are to rise above the average. It is this example that inspires and motivates other people to rise above their previous levels of accomplishment.

The fourth quality of motivational leadership is *realism*. Realism is a form of intellectual honesty. The realist insists upon seeing the world as it really is, not as he wishes it were. This objectivity, this refusal to engage in self-delusion, is a mark of the true leader.

Those who exhibit the quality of realism do not trust to luck, hope for miracles, pray for exceptions to basic business principles, expect rewards without working or hope that problems will go away by themselves. These all are examples of self-delusion, of living in a fantasyland. The motivational leader insists on seeing things exactly as they are and encourages others to look at life the same way.

The fifth quality of motivational leadership is *responsibility*. This is perhaps the hardest of all to develop. The acceptance of responsibility means that, as Harry Truman said, "The buck stops here."

The game of life is very competitive. Life is very much like competitive sports. Very small things that you do, or don't do, can either give you the edge that leads to victory or take away your edge at the critical moment. This principle is especially true with regard to accepting responsibility for yourself and for everything that happens to you.

Personal leadership and motivational leadership are very much the same. To lead others, you must first lead yourself. To be an example or a role model for others, you must first become an excellent person yourself.

You motivate yourself with a big vision, and as you move progressively toward its realization, you motivate and enthuse others to work with you to fulfill that vision.

You exhibit absolute honesty and integrity with everyone in everything you do. You are the kind of person others admire and respect and want to be like. You set a standard that others aspire to. You live in truth with yourself and others so that they feel confident giving you their support and their commitment.

You demonstrate courage in everything you do by facing doubts and uncertainties and moving forward regardless. You put up a good front even when you feel anxious about the outcome. You don't burden others with your fears and misgivings. You constantly push yourself out of your comfort zone and in the direction of your goals. And no matter how bleak the situation might appear, you keep on keeping on with a smile.

You are intensely realistic. You encourage others to be realistic and objective about their situations as well. You encourage them to realize and appreciate that there is a price to pay for everything they want. They have weaknesses that they will have to overcome, and they have standards that they will have to meet, if they want to survive and thrive in a competitive market.

You accept complete responsibility for results. You refuse to make excuses or blame others or hold grudges against people who you feel may have wronged you. You say, "If it's to be, it's up to me." You repeat over and over the words, "I am responsible. I am responsible. I am responsible."

Finally, you take action. You know that all mental preparation and character building is merely a prelude to action. It's not what you say but what you do that counts.

The mark of the true leader is that he or she leads the action. You become a motivational leader by motivating yourself. And you motivate yourself by striving toward excellence. You motivate yourself by throwing your whole heart into doing your job in an excellent fashion. You motivate yourself and others by continually looking for ways to help others to improve their lives and achieve their goals. You become a motivational leader by becoming the kind of person others want to get behind and support in every way.

Your main job is to take complete control of your personal evolution and become a leader in every area of your life. You could ask for nothing more, and you should settle for nothing less.

The master in the art of living
makes little distinction between his
work and his play, his labor
and his leisure, his mind and his body,
his information and his recreation,
his love and his religion.

He hardly knows which is which.

He simply pursues his vision of
excellence at whatever he does,
leaving others to decide whether
he is working or playing.

To him he's always doing both.

-James Michener

www.ThePowerOfCoaching.com

Denis Waitley

 Denis Waitley is a respected author, keynote speaker and productivity consultant on high performance human achievement. The following article was reproduced with permission from Denis Waitley's Weekly Ezine. To subscribe to Denis Waitley's Weekly Ezine, go to www.deniswaitley.com or send an email with the word "Join" in the subject line to subscribe@deniswaitley.com Copyright©2005 Denis Waitley International. All rights reserved worldwide.

Chapter Thirteen

BECOMING A PROACTIVE LEADER

Denis Waitley

The knowledge era's new leaders, many of whom are immigrants and women, are managing change by conceiving innovative organizations and novel ways to attract and motivate employees. They are learning to be proactive instead of reactive and to appreciate the full importance of relationships and alliances. They also have a healthy aptitude for risk and perseverance and know how to gain strength from setbacks and failure.

Life's Batting Average

Baseball's greatest hitter grew up near my neighborhood in San Diego. When Ted Williams slugged for the Boston Red Sox, my father and I kept a record of his daily batting average. And when I played Little League ball, my dad told me not to worry about striking out. In Williams's finest year, dad reminded me, the champion failed at the plate about 60 percent of the time.

Football's greatest quarterbacks complete only six out of ten passes. The best basketball players make only half their shots. Even with satellite mapping and expert geologists, leading oil companies make strikes in only one out of ten wells. Actors and actresses auditioning for roles are turned down twenty-nine in thirty times. And stock market winners make money on only two out of five of their investments.

Since failure is a given in life, success takes more than leadership beliefs and solid behavioral patterns. It also takes an appropriate response to the inevitable, including an effective combination of risk-taking and perseverance. I meet many individuals who are seeking security at all costs, and avoiding risk whenever and wherever possible. Knowing that certain changes would make success much more likely for them, they nevertheless take the path of least resistance: no change. For the temporary, often illusory, comfort of staying as they are, they pay the terrible price of a life not truly lived.

Parable of the Cautious Man

There was a very cautious man,
who never laughed or cried.
He never risked, he never lost,
he never won nor tried.
And when he one day passed away,
his insurance was denied,
For since he never really lived,
they claimed he never died.

In other words, missed opportunities are the curse of potential. After the Great Depression, Americans, perhaps understandably, took many steps intended to minimize risk. The government guaranteed much of our savings. Citizens bought billions of dollars worth of insurance. We sought lifetime employment, and our unions fought for guaranteed annual cost-of-living increases to protect us from inflation. This security-blanket mentality has continued in recent decades as executives awarded themselves golden parachutes in case a merger or takeover took their plum jobs.

These measures had many benefits, but the drawbacks have also been heavy, even if less obvious. In our eagerness to avoid risk, we forgot its positive aspects. Many of us continue to overlook the fact that progress comes only when chances are taken. And the security we sought and continue to seek often produces boredom, mediocrity, apathy and reduced opportunity. We still hear much about security, especially from federal and state politicians. But total security is a myth except, perhaps, for those six feet underground in the cemetery. We may, indeed, ask our government for guaranteed benefits. But we must be aware that when a structure starts with a *floor*, walls and ceilings will follow. And herein lies a paradoxical proverb:

You must risk in order to gain security, but you must never seek security.

When security becomes a major goal in life – when fulfillment and joy are reduced to merely holding on, sustaining the status quo – the risk remains heavy. It is then a risk of losing the prospects of real advancement, of not being able to ride the wave of change today and tomorrow. Had the founders of Yahoo, Amazon.com and America Online been concerned with immediate profits and return on investment, we would not be enjoying those Internet services today, each of which has a greater market capitalization than IBM or General Motors.

Procrastination Doesn't Make Perfect

Perfectionists are often great procrastinators. Having stalled until the last minutes, they tear into a project with dust flying and complaints about insufficient time. Perfectionist-procrastinators are masters of the excuse that short notice kept them from doing the quality job they *could* have done.

But that's hardly the only variety of procrastination – which is one of my own favorite hiding places when I try to blame external conditions instead of myself for some difficulty. Mine comes with a gnawing feeling of being fatigued, always behind. I try to tell myself that I'm taking it easy and gathering my energies for a big new push, but procrastination differs markedly from genuine relaxation – which is truly needed. And it saves me no time or energy. On the contrary, it drains both, leaving me with self-doubt on top of self-delusion.

We're all very busy. Every day we seem to have a giant to-do list of people to see, projects to complete, e-mails to read, e-mails to write. We have calls to answer and calls to make, then more calls to people with whom we keep playing voice-mail tag.

Henri Nouwen's classic book *Making All Things New* likens our lives to "overstuffed suitcases that are bursting at the seams." Feeling there is forever far too much to do, we say we're really under the gun this week. But working hard or even heroically to solve a problem is little to our credit if we created the problem in the first place. When most people refer to themselves as being under the gun, they want to believe, or *do* believe, that the pressures and problems are not of their own making. In most cases, however, the gun appeared after failure to attend to business in good time. Instead of being proactive early, they procrastinated until the due date became a crisis deadline.

By the Inch Life's a Cinch, by the Yard it's Hard

One of the best escapes from the prison of procrastination is to take even the smallest steps toward your goals. People usually procrastinate because of fear and lack of self-confidence – and, ironically, become even more afraid when under the gun. There are many ways to experiment and test new ground without risking the whole ball game on one play.

Experience has shown that when people go after one big goal at once, they invariably fail. If you had to swallow a twelve-ounce steak all at once, you'd choke. You have to cut the steak into small pieces, eating one bite at a time. So it is with prioritizing. Proactive goal achievement means taking every project and cutting it up into bite-sized pieces. Each small task or requirement on the way to the ultimate goal becomes a mini-goal in itself. Using this method, the goal becomes manageable. When mini-mistakes are made, they are easy to correct. And with the achievement of each mini-goal, you receive reinforcement and motivation in the form of positive feedback. As basic as this sounds, much frustration and failure is caused when people try to "bite off more than they can chew" by taking on assignments with limited resources and impossible timeline expectations.

Two major fears that sire procrastination are fear of the unknown and fear of rejection or looking foolish. A third fear – of success – is often overlooked. Many people, even many executives, fear success because it carries added responsibility that can seem too heavy to bear, such as setting an example of excellence that calls for additional effort and willingness to take risks. Success, without adequate self-esteem or the belief that it is deserved, also can create feelings of guilt, and the result is only temporary or fleeting high achievement. Playing it safe can seem more tempting than a need to step forward with determination to do it now and do it right.

Moving from Procrastination to Proactivation:

Here are some ideas to help make you a victor over change rather than a victim of change:

1. Set your wake-up time a half hour earlier tomorrow and keep the clock at that setting. Use the extra time to think about the best way to spend your day.

2. Memorize and repeat this motto: "Action TNT: Today, not Tomorrow." Handle each piece of incoming mail only once. Answer your e-mail either early in the morning or after working hours.

Block out specific times to initiate phone calls, personally take incoming calls, and to meet people in person.

3. When people tell you their problems, give solution-oriented feedback. Rather than taking on the problem as your own assignment, first, ask what's the next step they plan to take or what they would like to see happen.

4. Finish what you start. Concentrate all your energy and intensity without distraction on successfully completing your current major project.

5. Be constructively helpful instead of unhelpfully critical. Single out someone or something to praise instead of participating in group griping, grudge collecting or pity parties.

6. Limit your television viewing or Internet surfing to mostly educational or otherwise enlightening programs. Watch no more than one hour of television per day or night, unless there is a special program you have been anticipating. The Internet has also become a great procrastinator's hideout for tension-relieving instead of goal-achieving activities.

7. Make a list of five necessary but unpleasant projects you've been putting off, with a completion date for each project. Immediate action on unpleasant projects reduces stress and tension. It is very

difficult to be active and depressed at the same time.

8. Seek out and converse with a successful role model and mentor. Learning from others' successes and setbacks will inevitably improve production of any kind. Truly listen; really find out how your role models do it right.

9. Understand that fear, as an acronym, is False Evidence Appearing Real, and that luck could mean Laboring Under Correct Knowledge. The more information you have on any subject – especially case histories – the less likely you'll be to put off your decisions.

10. Accept problems as inevitable offshoots of change and progress. With the ever more rapid pace of change in society and business, you'll be overwhelmed unless you view change as normal and learn to look for its positive aspects – such as new opportunities and improvements – rather than bemoan the negative.

There is actually no such thing as a "future" decision; there are only present decisions that will affect the future. Procrastinators wait for just the right moment to decide.

If *you* wait for the prefect moment, you become a security-seeker who is running in place, unwittingly digging yourself deeper into your rut. If you wait for every objection to be overcome, you'll attempt nothing.

Get out of your comfort zone and go from procrastinating to proactivating. Make your personal motto: "Stop stewing and start doing!"

Renate de Angelo

 With over 12 years working as a master certified coach through the International Coaches Federation, Renate's mission is to coach, inspire and train leaders to "Awaken the Leader Within." Renate currently coaches, trains and mentors people to become professional life and business coaches. She is the owner and president of "Dimension Coaching & Training"™ programs designed for individuals and companies to achieve inspired performance and to create a compelling future for themselves and their organization. For more information, visit her website at DimensionCoachTraining.com or call 916-481-4473.

Chapter Fourteen

AWAKEN THE LEADER WITHIN

THE LEADERSHIP JOURNEY

Renate de Angelo

O ne day, I came across a story that shifted the way I look at life, relationships, and business forever:

A beggar had been sitting by the side of the road for over 30 years. One day, a stranger walked by. "Spare some change?" mumbled the beggar, holding out his hand. "I have nothing to give you," said the stranger. Then the stranger asked, "What's that you are sitting on?"

"Nothing," replied the beggar. "Just an old box, I have been sitting on it for as long as I can remember." "Ever looked inside?" asked the stranger.

"No," said the beggar. "What's the point? There is nothing in there." "Have a look inside," insisted the stranger.

The beggar managed to pry open the lid. To his astonishment, disbelief, he saw that the box was filled with gold.

Through this story, I recognized that each journey to greatness, personal as well as professional, starts from within. Everything I had been searching for was already within my reach, waiting to be discovered.

How can YOU discover the breakthrough secrets that are hidden in the "old box" you have been sitting on for so long? When will you uncover your personal Power, skyrocket your Self-Confidence, burst all your Limiting Beliefs, and propel your life to Inner Peace, Abundance, Fulfillment, Gratitude, Joy, and Success?

Do you believe that you can have it all? What is holding you back from living your greatness? When will your "greater" part rule above the "smaller" part of you? What would it take for you to start your Leadership Journey today? Come and find out for yourself!

At the core of my coaching practice is the belief that unlimited potential resides in each and every person, and that this potential is revealed by being true to yourself and living your truth with others. This means walking your own path -- not someone else's or a path someone else thinks you should take. Each of us is unique and gifted. When each of us search within ourselves, honestly acknowledging our strengths and weaknesses, our individual paths will become clear.

For my coaching clients and those I train to become life or business coaches, I am that stranger urging each individual to look inside of their own "box" of untapped resources and possibilities and helping them discover what is holding them back so they finally have the courage to open the box and go for the gold. Success is always ours to enjoy when we keep what it is that we do best and let others do the same.

All too well, we know that every limitation is self-imposed; we are all ordinary until we decide to be extraordinary. As coaches, we lead our clients on that journey to go for the gold, to uncover their unique gifts and to awaken the Leader within, so that they can live extraordinary lives. That is what the leadership journey is all about.

Successful coaches must first walk that journey themselves. Your success on the leadership journey is relative, and only you can envision and decide how far you want to go. In order to achieve long-term success, you will need a strong internal partnership based on:

- knowing who you are,
- knowing what you want, and
- knowing where you want to go in life.

When we begin to walk that journey, knowing who we are, why we are here and how we want to share our gifts with others, we set the foundation for our future work with clients. We live by example, into our vision and help others to do the same.

What is your vision? Why are you here? As human beings, we either live from our VISION or from our STORIES.

The VISION is what you came to do.

The STORY is what you tell yourself and others why you cannot do it, why you don't have it (Fear, Limiting Belief…), etc.

As coaches, our purpose is to reconnect our client to their Vision. Every business, scientific or medical discovery, and product that exists today was at some time in history a vision, "impossible." Victory is yours only when you can envision it, believe it, see it, smell it, taste it, hear it, and feel it!

It is crucial that an Awakened Leader create that vision within themselves. If you can't see yourself winning that award and feel the tears of triumph streaming down your face, it's unlikely you will be able to lead yourself or others to victory.

Vision without action is a daydream, and action without vision is a nightmare. -Japanese proverb

We spend a lifetime trying to understand who we are, becoming more aware and finding a balance between body, mind and spirit.

As everything in our world is governed by laws, we are governed by physical, as well as spiritual, laws. We are very familiar with the physical laws – getting a speeding ticket, the law of gravity, knowing when we drop something it will fall. How familiar are you with the spiritual laws that govern our Universe?

For example, one of the spiritual laws is the Law of Attraction – the most important law of the universe. We attract into our life what we focus on. Another one is the law of Cause and Effect, which states that every action has an equal reaction! Therefore, every cause must have an effect, and every effect must have a cause.

Thoughts are causal in nature, so every thought has an effect in the physical world in which we live. If we are conscious or unconscious about what we are thinking, we create our world according to our thoughts.

These laws exist and surround us; they are always at work whether we believe in them or not.

- What are your thoughts in regard to your life?
- What kind of life would you like to live?
- What is life asking you to do differently?
- What would you be doing in the presence of fearlessness?
- What would you change in your current life if you had the courage?
- What kind of life would you live, if you would give yourself permission to be happy and enjoy life?

It starts with our thoughts, our state of Being (Cause) knowing who we are and why we are here, to move into the state of Doing (Effect) to create and manifest what we want and to share our gifts with others.

Just as there are physical and spiritual laws, each of us have a physical and spiritual component. I refer to these as states of Being and Doing. Inner fulfillment and outer success is a very fine balancing act between the state of Being and the state of Doing.

Most often, we get lost in "Doing" and disconnect with our inner core essence and truth. That is when the trouble starts. When this happens, you disconnect from your authentic self and you focus more and more on external goals, such as owning a bigger house or car. When living in that state of Doing, we live in our mind, in a state of duality, of having "not enough," competition and wants.

The importance is to find a proper balance, because if your focus is exclusively on the state of Being, you will be disconnected from the physical world of manifesting. None of these are good or bad on their own; it simply is that we need both. The key is to find the empowering balance.

When we live from the state of Being, we connect with Spirit, the state of oneness, and of possibilities. Our focus goes within, and we are connected to that internal stillness that has no form and is the place of creativity. Beingness is a place from which we come, rather than a place we go to. It is the essence of who we are - spiritual Beings with unlimited Potential and energy; eternal Beings, creator of visions and possibilities.

When you recognize the difference between those two realities and learn to live in both worlds, mastering the ability to switch back and forth, then you have found the balance between Being and Doing, and you shift from needing to control life to a mastery of life. You will be awakened and connected with the Leader within.

We are called BE-INGS, not DO-INGS.

This important principle of balance between Being and Doing is crucial to the act of successful coaching. In order to awaken the leader within each of our clients, we must help them to connect with that place within where all things originate from, to emanate from that place of power to create and manifest, and encourage them to return to that place within themselves.

On the "Doing" Side

Coaching is all about assisting people in setting goals, stretching their minds, creating roadmaps on how to get there, using the client's talents and skills, as well as inspiring them to create extraordinary results. We, as coaches, open possibilities for our clients to learn, to master concepts and strategies, and to establish well-defined goals in order for them to create extraordinary results in their personal as well as professional lives.

On the "Being" Side

The act of coaching is to tap into each individual's pathway and purpose through processes that reconnect and unlock the client's gifts and talents, so they can create and sustain successful, life-changing behaviors.

It takes courage for you to step outside your comfort zone into your vision, the unknown; to bring awareness and learning, discovering more about yourself, being more transparent, willing to be transformed, and being reinvented daily to become who you are meant to be.

You will know when your client has found that balance because they will have learned to be at ease with 'not knowing' and to trust from that inner core of their Being. We, then, have tapped into something beyond our Doing, for we have connected with infinite power, an energy bigger than life itself.

How do you get there? How do you awaken the Leader within? It will require you as the coach to ask very deep, probing, inquiring questions in order to create trust in your client to be open, encouraging her/him to see familiar things in different ways, and to create the foundation to allow truthful answers to emerge.

Many of you will say, "I am not ready; I don't know where to start." You think there must be a magic formula. Or, you come up with reasons why you can't do it, encountering oppositions, challenges, and adversities. You say: "If I could eliminate all that, I could do it."

Just remember: You are never ready – and it's never convenient to start the journey.

The question to be answered truthfully by you as a coach, as well as each of your clients, is:

"Who are you willing to become in the face of adversity?"

ADVERSITY 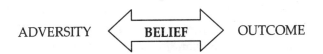 OUTCOME

When adversity comes up, it doesn't lead automatically to an outcome. In between every adversity and every outcome is your belief. Your belief, which is the driving force, affects the final outcome. What is the source of your belief? Are you coming from a place of fear or love?

Fear is a death sentence on the path to achievement. We are afraid to stand out, speak our minds, or take a risk because we are afraid of being criticized or looking foolish. It is Fear that stops us from being the leaders in our own lives today and tomorrow. Fear creates a negative vision of the future; it's disempowering and non supportive.

Love infuses your vision of the future positively; it empowers and supports.

Find out for yourself:

- **Who am I in this situation?**
  (FEAR based: angry, frustrated –LOVE based: kind, respectful)

- **What do I hold on to?**
  (FEAR based: power, being right – LOVE based: unconditional love, respect, integrity)

- **What am I willing to let go of?**
  (behaviors that don't serve me any longer)

- **Who am I willing to Be in order to become 'that'?**
  (supportive behaviors like respectful, team player, truthful)

- **What am I committed to, in order to create the desired outcome?**

- **What is my next step?**

YOU ARE THE STAR – be the awakened leader in your own world first, walking your own transformational journey. Then, you will achieve the outcomes you are looking for by being the change you want to see in your life, company, and in the world.

A leader is created daily, not in a day!

Don Boyer

Don Boyer, creator of the best-selling The Power of Mentorship series, is an outstanding speaker and a proficient published author. His mission, passion and purpose are to help you reach your full potential. He is a proud father and grandfather and resides in Southern California with his wonderful wife, Melinda. You can contact Don by sending an email to him at donboyer@realifeteaching.com or don@donboyer.org. He can also be contacted by telephone at 562-789-1909. Visit his website at www.realifeteaching.com.

Chapter Fifteen

ROAD MAP TO SUCCESS

Don Boyer

H ave you ever wondered how to go from where you currently are to where you want to be? First, you need to find out what you really want, who you want to become and what you want to do. Once you have that figured out, you are well on your way to the land of achievement. I am going to share with you seven of the most powerful secrets on the planet to help you reach the next level of success.

Mentorship secret number one is to choose those you associate with very wisely. It is a fact that you become like the people in your inner circle. If you hang around with nine broke friends, you are sure to be the tenth. The only way you will ever rise in character, finances and overall success is to associate with individuals who have already attained what you desire. That is why having a mentor or a circle of mentors is so important.

Listen, your success and achievement are not celebrated by the group called 'average', but in the encampment of winners. Those who have what you want are the ones who will cheer for you and help you up the ladder of success. The group called 'average' believes the only way they can make it up the ladder is by pulling you down the ladder. You may love "Know-it-All Rudy," but if he is a hindrance to your success... Rudy has to go! No matter what you want to achieve in life, there is a mentor out there who wants to help you reach your dreams. Take inventory of your life today, and see who is in your inner circle. Then, make the necessary change.

Mentorship secret number two is guard your thoughts. Most people have no clue how powerful their thoughts are and what results they bring. Everything you have in your life, good or bad, is a result of your conscious or subconscious thoughts. No one has ever achieved mega-success and reached their dreams without constantly thinking about it for months, and, most likely, for years.

Train yourself to think thoughts of success, increase, prosperity, and favor; and it won't be long before these things start showing up in your life. You can change your life by changing your thoughts. Only you have the power to choose your thoughts; so, like those you associate with, choose your thoughts...wisely.

Mentorship secret number three is to build a million dollar vocabulary. I am not talking about learning fancy words that only a scholar would understand or appreciate (although good language and excellent words are invaluable). No, what I mean is to use words that are full of life, power and energy. Hey, you cannot afford the luxury and comfort of using negative words. Those kind of words will keep you broke, defeated and in a constant state of failure.

Like your associates and thoughts, you must choose wisely the words that flow from your lips. Words, the experts tell us, contain the power to create life and death. You are speaking words that are creating your success and prosperity or words that are destroying it. There are no such things as "empty words." All words contain power - life-changing, destiny-altering, and mountain-moving or mountain-staying power. What you say is what you get. Do I mean that by saying, "I am going to be a millionaire," that I will cause it to happen? No, not if every word after that is, "I am so broke, I can't even pay attention." Positive words, life-changing words, are not a one-time event but a lifestyle.

If being a millionaire is one of your dreams and you choose the right associates, master your thoughts and words, then that dream or any other dream can be attained. Okay, is the road map to success easy? Yes, it is. Poverty, lack, broken relationships, and failure – those are the hard roads. Will it take work? You bet it will, but you can have a blast while in training. No farmer ever had a great harvest without a lot of work. But, during reaping season when the harvest came in, that old farmer would look back with a smile on his face and a prayer of thanksgiving in his heart and say, "It was worth it."

Mentorship secret number four is understanding and using the law of the harvest. Everything in life is based on cause and effect, on sowing and reaping. One of the biggest mistakes people make is thinking that they can get something for nothing. Ask any sane person if they believe they can get something for nothing; they would say no. Yet, millions of people everyday live out their lives in this very pattern. Life is full of abundance; there is no such thing as shortage. Shortage is made by man from his lack of understanding how life really works.

If you want more of something, the starting point is to give first. Whatever you sow or give will come back to you multiplied. That is how life works, and it is based on the same reliable laws that make the sun rise in the morning and the moon shine at night. It works 100% of the time. Do you ever wake up in the morning thinking that the law of gravity is not going to work and you will fly off the planet? Of course not, that kind of thought never enters your mind. The reason why you never think that kind of thought is the law of gravity works no matter what you do or what you believe about it. It works because that is the way life designed it to work and it is not based on what man does.

The law of the harvest works the exact same way. When you sow or give, it always comes back to you...multiplied. People use this law backwards. They take from life and people thinking that is the way to get more; but the law of sowing and reaping kicks in, and, instead of gaining more, they lose more. They sow seeds of taking away, and the law comes back multiplied and takes more from them. Always remember the key to having more is by giving first. It is one of grandest laws of success life has given to mankind. The law of life says it so well, "Give and it shall be given to you in good measure; pressed down and shaken together will men give to you."

Mentorship secret number five is working the law of the millionaire. What is the law of the millionaire? It is a law that has created more millionaires throughout the ages than maybe any other law known to man. It is a law that made J.C Penny a very wealthy man. John D. Rockefeller, Sr., used this law not only to create a fortune in assets, but he also used it to extend his life. In his forties, the best medical doctors of his time gave him only a short time to live due to an incurable disease. He applied this law to his health and lived into his nineties. Financial tycoons like Alexander Kerr and John Templeton attribute their wealth to this law. Is this some modern insight or newly discovered law of the 19th, 20th, or 21st century? Heavens no, it goes back to the beginning of time. It made men like Abraham very rich in gold, silver, cattle and land. It made King Solomon so rich that a queen fainted when she viewed all his wealth.

Are you chomping at the bit to find out what this law is? Are you asking if you could use this law and gain the same results as these other men? The answer is yes you can use this law and gain the same results. This grand law I am talking about is the law of tithing. Giving away 10% of your income will create untold wealth and goodness in your life. Men throughout centuries have proven that this law is true. The results are not based on theory or speculation but on proven facts based on law or principle. You want to create an extraordinary amount of wealth into your life? Implement the law of tithing and prove it yourself.

Mentorship secret number six is using the power of affirmations. You can create any lifestyle, make any improvements, and even change your destiny by the use of affirmations. Affirmations help take you from where you are at to where you want to go. They are the bridge that allows your hope to cross over to become your manifested dream. As you speak the things you want to have, the person you want to become, and the way things are going to be, you are molding your future. "Can this be true?" you ask. Doesn't life work by chance or fate or luck? No, life is based on law and principle. As you apply affirmations to your life, you are changing what is to what will be.

It will take some time and consistent persistence on your part, and your inner thoughts may make you feel like you are lying, but that is only from never being taught the truth of affirmations and how life works. Once you understand how life responds to affirmations and know their power, those uncomfortable feelings will disappear. The results you will receive from affirmations will be well worth any price of discipline you must pay. Write down what you want, who you want to become and say it out loud everyday!

Mentorship secret number seven is to practice the three C's of success: Take charge - take control - take a chance. The power that fuels these three C's is action. You can have dreams, set goals and even have a business plan in writing, but without action, it is only self deception. Action is the key ingredient that separates those who reach their dreams and those who don't. Will you dream of achievements or achieve your dream? The answer to that question is found in action or the lack of it. Whatever your dream is, take charge, take action. You want to reach your goal? Take control by taking action. Will you live out and achieve your dreams? You can by taking a chance and taking action towards it.

You have two choices in life - you can accept the way things are or take the responsibility to change them. The great mentor Jim Rohn says that the greatest sign of maturity is to make no excuses when your harvest is small and no apologies when your harvest is great. This means that success or failure cannot be blamed on people, circumstances, or any other outside force, but is a direct result of what we do...or don't do. If you are going to reach your dreams and achieve all things you want, it will because you do the things that will bring those results. In order to receive the things desired, you must sow the seeds required. Everyone wants success; they want more money, better jobs, and great relationships, but the sad fact is only 3% or less of the people who say they want success will do the things that will bring it. Why is this? You have to put this question to one of the great wonders of the world; it just doesn't make any sense. Failure is a much harder and higher price to pay than success. Okay, now that you know the road map to success, what are waiting for? Get up and get going, and I will see you in the land of abundance.

Robert J. Fashano

Robert J. Fashano, CLU, ChFC, MSFS, has been a General Agent for The Guardian since 1979 in Buffalo, New York. Within The Guardian, he has served on the Field Advisory Board and served as Chairman in 1997 and 1998. Bob has spoken throughout the country to industry and non-industry groups. Currently he serves on GAMA's Foundation Board of Trustees and is Fundraising Chairman. He is married to his high school sweetheart of 41 years, and they have two children, both of whom are in the business. Contact Robert at 800-777-3411, email rfashano@allianceadvisorygroup.com or visit www.allianceadvisorygroup.com.

Chapter Sixteen

GROW THE PEOPLE, THEY WILL GROW THE BUSINESS

Robert J. Fashano

The Leader as Coach

As a leader, we have many responsibilities and wear several hats. I have learned the number one priority in building the business is helping the key people grow.

Coaching and mentoring key management and top producers will always produce results. In addition, you receive great satisfaction from having a part in the growth of an individual.

In my view, the single most important asset in any organization is the key people. In an agency, clearly the management and top producers are the most valuable asset. The growth of the firm is in direct proportion to the growth of these people.

Effective coaching begins by seeing greatness in people and helping them discover it. The German writer, Goethe, wrote, "Treat people as if they were what they ought to be, and you help them become what they are capable of being."

The Coaching and Counseling Process

Your belief in people will strongly influence them. I firmly believe that the following three factors influence people's performance:

1. To the degree that you sincerely believe that they can achieve higher productivity.

2. To the degree they believe that you believe that.

3. To the degree that there is trust, mutual respect and rapport between you and them.

Your genuine concern and sincere interest in people and in helping them reach their goals will add to your coaching sessions.

Here are some tips I have found effective in coaching sessions:

    a) Coach in a private room
    b) Allow no calls or interruptions
    c) Listen more than preach
    d) Look for their strengths
    e) Seek to understand them

The following coaching process is a guide to assist you to more meaningful coaching sessions:

1. **ASK** about goals and objectives.
    *   "What specific goals are you working on? Where are you in respect to them?"

- "What's in the way and keeping you from reaching the goals?"
- "What strengths, skills, or activities will help you overcome these obstacles?"
- "What is your action plan?"

2. **LISTEN** without distractions or interruptions
    - Listen to people's words, tone of voice and body language.
    - Guide and question them – help them discover their own answers (beware of the Monkey - more on that later).

3. **COACH** knowledge, skills or actions
    - Address problem issues or areas of improvement.
    - Suggest one action that will help remove an obstacle or move toward a goal.
    - Keep the responsibility on their shoulders – not yours (beware of the Monkey).

4. **PRAISE** behaviors
    - Point out specific talents, skills, attitudes, knowledge they have.
    - Express potential they have for growth that they might not see in themselves.

5. **CHALLENGE** them to be their best
    - Ask them to commit to specific goals, results and time frames.

Monkey Business is Bad Business

Always *beware of the Monkey.* The Monkey looks cute, innocent, and fun loving. In this case, the Monkey can be dangerous.

As stated previously, our priority is to grow our people. In this process, it can become easy for you to accept their challenges and issues and try to solve them. Let's talk about the Monkey to help make the point. Let me set the stage:

You are alone in your office, or you could be walking down the hall. An associate, member of management or a staff person suddenly approaches you. Then, comes a <u>question</u> and their <u>statement</u>. <u>Question</u>: "Bob, do you have a moment?" *Careful – here it comes – Monkey transfer begins.* You answer, "Yes." *Transfer complete.* <u>Statement</u>: "Bob, I have a problem, " or "We have an issue," or "I need you to help with _____."

When you now begin the discussion and enter into problem solving, often you run out of time. He or she innocently has left you his/her Monkey. Another meeting must be arranged, or you need to do research to help the situation.

Whatever the situation, you simply cannot end the meeting with their Monkey. If you take their Monkey, they don't grow. Over the years, I have taken my share of other people's Monkeys. I felt, "I am supposed to have all the answers. I have all these initials after my name. I have all this experience. They expect to come to me for solutions." I wasn't leading; I was being lead. I wasn't proactive; I was reactive. You see, when you get close to people in a coaching session, there is a risk of taking their Monkey. I simply have no more time for other people's Monkeys. I have all the time in the world for them (especially top performers), but no time for their Monkeys.

You may wish to try this technique when you have an unexpected visit. You are in your office, and you invite them in – immediately <u>stand up</u>. This action alone suggests a quickie ("no way am I taking your Monkey standing up.") Listen, and if need be, schedule a coaching session. It is during a coaching session when you can effectively ask questions and guide them to solve their problem.

The best advice I have seen on this subject is in an old Chinese psalm written by Lao Tzu. It says, "Go to the people; live among them; love them; learn from them; start from where they are; work with them; build on what they have; but of the best leaders, when the task is accomplished, the work completed, the people will remark: *"we have done it ourselves.""*

There is Power in the Questions

One of author Steven Covey's habits in *The Seven Habits of Highly Successful People* is to "Seek first to understand, then to be understood." As a mentor-coach, there exists the temptation to tell, talk too much, preach, etc. The intention is to change behavior and increase performance. However, I've learned the real art in developing people is allowing them to discover for themselves. This is best done with power questions.

Always probe to make certain you're focusing on the right issue. Some tips may help:

- Ask questions that contain the words who, what, where, why, when, and how.
- These questions should call for responses, not just yes or no answers.
- Avoid questions with hidden solutions like, "Have you tried x, y, z yet?"
- Avoid multiple-choice questions such as, "What do you think is going on – is it ____ or is it ____?" Don't offer solutions in your questions.

Sample Power Questions

Obviously, the question is based on the frequency of your coaching sessions. In addition, issues and challenges will dictate the form of questioning. Below are some examples:

- What is your desired outcome?
- What have you already tried?
- How is this issue/problem affecting you?
- Why is this important to you?
- What would be the financial impact if this were resolved?
- What would you be willing to do to change the situation?
- What would it look like when it is accomplished?

Questions relating to their goals:

- Where are you now, in relation to where you want to go?
- What are some specific activities you are willing to commit to toward achieving your goals?
- What is in the way of you achieving this goal?
- What new skills or knowledge is needed?
- What new habits are required?

These are just a few examples. I'm sure you can add more. Your role in the process is to inquire and stimulate thought-invoking problem solving on their part. I have found in almost 100% of the cases that they have the answers and solutions. Remember, this is a coaching session – not a training session. When they discover for themselves, the how-to change can take place.

Being an active listener in these sessions is also important. As a reminder:

- Maintain eye contact
- Smile at appropriate moments
- Avoid distractions
- Take notes only when necessary
- Be sensitive to body language
- Listen first and evaluate later
- Never interrupt except to ask for clarification
- Occasionally repeat what was said

See Yourself as Their Strategic Partner

As a coach-mentor, you partner with them in their growth and development. You play a key role in guiding them through their challenges, issues, goal achievement, etc.

An often accepted definition of leadership is *influence*. The responsibility of leadership is growing and developing people, in particular, your key people. What I am learning is that people become what the most important people in their lives think they will become. Henry Ford said it best when he said, "My best friend is the one who brings out the best in me."

Andrew Carnegie at one time was the wealthiest man in America. He came to this country from native Scotland as a small boy. He performed odd jobs and eventually headed up the largest steel manufacturer in the world. At one time, he had 43 millionaires working for him. That may not seem like much, but in those days that was a rare commodity, a millionaire. In fact, I would dare say it's probably the equivalent of 20 million today. A reporter was interviewing Andrew Carnegie and the reporter said to him, "Mr. Carnegie, how did you hire 43 millionaires?" He said, "Well, you know, they weren't millionaires when I hired them." The reporter said, "Well, then how did you develop these people to the point where you would pay them so much money that they would amass this much wealth?" Carnegie replied, "Men are developed the same way gold is mined. When gold is mined, several tons of dirt must be moved to discover one ounce of

162

gold. But one doesn't go into the mine looking for dirt. One goes in looking for gold." That's how people are developed.

There is no doubt about it, people development and effective coaching takes time. It is becoming increasingly difficult with other pressing matters to dismiss people development. Performers and management teams are your most important asset. Therefore, it would be the best investment of our time.
In the end, coaching and mentoring another person is about changing their <u>thinking</u>. When you change thinking, you change <u>beliefs</u>. When you change beliefs, you can change their <u>expectations</u>. When you change expectations, you change <u>attitudes</u>. When you change attitudes, you can change their <u>behavior</u>. When behavior is changed, you change <u>performance</u>; and when you change performance, you can change a *life*.

We have an opportunity as leaders, as a coach and mentor, to make a difference in the life of another.

Seize the opportunity, cherish it, embrace it.

Chapter Seventeen

QUESTIONS ARE THE ANSWER

Machen MacDonald

I f you look up the word "coach" in the dictionary, the definition is: A large covered four wheel carriage used to transport people from one place to another. If you think about the job or role of a coach, it is still a vehicle by which you help transport a person from where they are to where they want to be. Throughout this book, you have gained various perspectives of how to engage excellence and move people from where they are to where they want to be. The magic of moving people to the achievement of their vision while on purpose is to help them gain the most empowering perspective. Therefore, the foundational "what" is perspective. The foundational "how" is through questions.

Here is a collection of questions which you can draw from and master to engage excellence in others. Peruse these questions before your coaching sessions and notice which ones seem to pop for you. Trust that you will gravitate toward the ones that are appropriate. Be aware that sometimes the people you lead may not want coaching in every situation. They may just be looking to vent. They may be seeking instruction or direction. Or, they may be looking to share a win. So, the most important first question to ask is: Do you want some coaching on that? And, then honor their response. If you are conducting a regularly scheduled coaching session, I suggest you choose from these great session starting questions:

- What's going great since we last talked?
- What would you like to talk about?
- How was your week?
- What should we make sure we focus on today?

To help you remember the types of questions you can ask to conduct meaningful coaching sessions, I came up with the acronym: **CURIOSITY CAP**. Be sure to put on your **CURIOSITY CAP** when you are coaching.

CURIOSITY	**CAP**
Clarifying	**C**hallenge
Understanding	**A**ttitude
Ready	**P**erspective
In the way	
Objective	
Strategy	
Insight	
Time	
Yes	

Clarifying Questions
These questions help you to see what is really going on and cut through the judgment, stories and drama that hold people back.

- What do you mean?
- What caused it?
- How did you get to this point?
- When does this happen?
- What have you tried so far?
- What do you think that means?
- What is this costing you?
- What is underneath that?
- What happened?
- What are you avoiding?
- What consequences are you avoiding?
- What are you denying yourself right now?
- What is the truth?
- What is important about that?
- What are you not saying?
- What else do you have to say about that?
- Can you say more about that?
- What are you not facing?
- What is your assessment?
- Is this good, bad, or in between? In what way?
- Will you give me an example?
- For instance?
- What would it look like?

Understanding Questions
These questions help coaches to discover the true goals, desires and objectives of their clients.

- What do you want?
- What is your key goal?

- Do you want to adjust your goal?
- May we explore that some more?
- If you got that, what would you have? Or, what would that give you?
- What are you committed to?
- What is your motivation for hitting your goal?
- What is the dream?
- What is your big game?
- How will you know if you have reached it?
- What is beyond this problem?
- What is ahead?
- What are you building towards?
- What has to happen in order for you to feel successful?
- What is your gift/genius/brilliance that you can bring to this?
- What do you have invested in continuing to do it this way?

Ready Questions

Often, people get stuck because they are not clear on what their next steps are, and they have no awareness around their skill set or willingness to move forward. These questions help to determine what development needs to take place in order to keep making progress.

- What do you need in order to do this?
- What do you need to do so you can feel confident and get this done?
- Are you willing to do this?
- What are you willing to give up?
- What do you need to say "no" to?
- What do you need to say "yes" to?
- Do you feel prepared?

Ready Questions Continued:
- Is there anything you need to do to prepare for this? What is it?
- What do you need to put in place in order to accomplish this?
- What resources do you need to help you decide?
- How can you find out more about it?
- What resources are available to you?
- How could you adjust your environments to help support you with this?

In-the-Way Questions
These questions help one to see what they perceive to be in their way as they stray from their vision. Asking these types of questions minimizes or eliminates the overwhelm people feel so they can move around, over, under, or through the perceived obstacle.
- What is in your way?
- What is stopping you?
- What prevents you from handling this?
- What is holding you back?
- What would happen if…?
- What mistakes might you make?
- What seems to be the trouble?
- What seems to be the main obstacle?
- What concerns you the most about this?
- What are you afraid of?
- What is the worst that could happen?

Objective Questions
These questions increase objective awareness of limiting judgments and opinions which cause people to act and

behave in a way that may not be in alignment with their values or purpose.

- What's the judgment around that?
- What was the basis of that judgment?
- How did that judgment shape the relationship?
- What was done to trigger that reaction?
- Was it intended to bring about that reaction/ response? If yes, for what purpose?
- What was the expectation of others?
- What information or data are you choosing to ignore?
- What do you hope to accomplish by doing that?
- What is your heart telling you?
- What if you knew?

Strategy Questions

An effective coaching session ultimately results in creating or increasing an awareness and moving the objective forward. These questions will make sure that actions are taken in order to accomplish the defined objectives.

- What is your plan?
- What is your first step?
- What will you have to do to get the job done?
- What support do you need to accomplish this?
- What is the right action?
- What type of plan do you need to create?
- How do you suppose you could improve the situation?
- What are you going to do?
- What is left to do to have this be complete?
- What comes first?
- So what? Now what?

Strategy Questions Continued

- What action will you take? And after that?
- Is this a time for action? What action?
- Where do you go from here? When will you do that?
- What are your next steps?
- What can you use as leverage to make sure you follow through?
- What is the four-box model for gaining clarity with this?
- How can you set up an accountability mechanism?
- What activity are you going to change to alter the result that you've been getting?
- What action could you take that would be in alignment with your values?
- Does that decision give you peace or take your peace away?
- Is that contributing or contaminating your energy toward that?
- Are you inspired by taking that action?

Insight Questions

Many people are much more resourceful than they take credit for. These questions will play into that and tap their inner wisdom and promote their thinking process. These questions also serve to help people calibrate from the coaching and be more aware of what they are learning.

- What would you do differently?
- What haven't I asked that I should ask?
- What needs to be said that has not been said?
- What is the value you received from this meeting/conversation?

- What are you learning about yourself?
- What would you do differently if you tapped into your own wisdom?
- What are you noticing or becoming aware of?
- What is the simplest solution here?
- If I was experiencing this and you were the coach, what would you tell me?
- What will you take away from this?
- What could you learn or what skills will you acquire if you do this well?
- What was the lesson?
- How can you lock in the learning?
- How would you pull all of this together?
- What is your conclusion?
- What do you think this all amounts to?
- How would you summarize the effort so far?

Time Questions

These are important questions to ask at the conclusion of any coaching session in order to build commitment and accountability. As a coach, you also want to realize that a person may need to increase their bandwidth with regards to time. These questions will help you keep those you are coaching grounded and make them aware of realistic accomplishments given the timeframes involved.

- By when do you want to have this completed?
- How will you make the time to get this accomplished?
- How will you do this and still have time to meet your other objectives?

Time Questions Continued

- What activities might you need to defer or eliminate to stay on track with this?
- When will you do it?

Yes Questions

These are questions that are all about possibility. Help people step into their possibilities and magnificence.

- What will it look like when you succeed?
- What if there were no limits?
- What would help you know that I support this/you completely?
- Who do you need buy-in from in order to keep moving on this?
- What is the ideal outcome?
- What would you do if you knew you would not fail?
- What is your vision for yourself and the people around you?
- What is just one more possibility?
- How do you suppose it will all work out?
- What will that get you?
- What is your biggest strength?
- What are three creative things you could do to solve this?

Challenge Questions

These questions are used to get a person to step up and take things to the next level.

- Are you willing to do (action needed to be taken to move in desired direction)?
- Will you commit to doing (twice as much as they think they can)?

- What would you commit to doing if you were serious about your success?
- If your life depended on taking action, what would you do?
- If you had free choice in the matter, what would you do?
- If you could wipe the slate clean, what would you do?
- What steps do you commit to taking?

Attitude Questions

These questions will help people tap into how they must be in order to accomplish what they want for themselves.

- How do you want to be with this?
- How do you imagine (hero/mentor) approaching this?
- What part of you do you want to bring forward to accomplish this?
- What part of you do you want to see more of?
- What is working for you?
- What decision would you make from a position of strength?
- Who do you need to be in order to accomplish this?

Perspective Questions

These questions are intended to find out the current perspective from which the person you are coaching is coming from and also to get them to see other perspectives from which they can approach a situation.

Perspective Questions Continued

- What is the benefit or payoff in this situation or circumstance?
- What do you expect to happen?
- What other choices do you have?
- What is motivating you?
- What is missing here?
- What does this remind you of?
- How does it look to you?
- How do you feel about it?
- How can you have it be fun?
- What other angles can you think of?
- What's another way of looking at this?
- How else could a person handle this?
- What will open up for you when you get this resolved?
- What would you think about this five years from now?
- How does this relate to your values or life purpose?
- What is the worst and the best that could happen?
- In the bigger scheme of things, how important is this?
- So what?

"He who answers with a question makes those around him the wiser."   Anonymous

Download a free copy of these questions by visiting
www.ThePowerOfCoaching.com

Chapter Eighteen

WHAT IF EINSTEIN WAS YOUR COACH?

Machen MacDonald

E=MC²

Execution = Mentors X (Coaches Coaching)

C an you imagine tapping into the wisdom of one of the greatest minds the world has ever known? Some believe we can. Now, you can, too.

Among other axioms, Einstein is remembered for stating, "We can't solve problems by using the same kind of thinking we used when we created them." This is coaching at its core. It is imperative to have the willingness to explore new perspectives of how to see possibilities that exist which we just don't consciously see yet. In order to do this, you must often allow for the emotions of confusion, awkwardness, and frustration to show up in your experience. Sometimes you might need to get just downright messy.

To experience high caliber performance on game day, you must physically, mentally, and emotionally commit yourself in practice. Do not be encumbered with those who ridicule your performance on the field, for you are on the field and they are not. Mistakes, blunders and absurdities will creep in. This forges experience and character. Be willing to get it wrong; to screw it up. The willingness alone escorts you through to a higher level of excellence. By doing so, you are sure to unearth the solution and add to your bank of wisdom. This will serve to show the way to all who you affect. As Einstein says, "Anyone who has never made a mistake has never tried anything new." Where would we be if all those before us played it safe? What are you making way for by playing full out?

In quantum physics, it is accepted that whatever we focus on expands; or another way of saying it is, whatever we say to ourselves before we look at something determines what we see. We must then seek the proper perspective that will help us help others, as well as ourselves. When Coach Einstein proclaimed, "The most important decision we make is whether we believe we live in a friendly or hostile universe," he was pointing out the power of our beliefs and chosen perspectives and how they impact our experience of reality.

There are only two ways to live your life. One is as though nothing is a miracle. The other is as though everything is a miracle. The choice is yours to make.
                                              -Albert Einstein

You see, if you have the belief that things are tough, there's not enough time, people will let you down, you can't trust people or the company just doesn't care anymore, then you will only consciously see the evidence that supports those perspectives. Whereas, if you decide to become what I call an inverse paranoid, i.e., believe that people are out to help you and that the world is out to support you and all we have is time, then you start to consciously see all the evidence to sustain this reality.

To get this, you may need to suspend what you believe to be current reality. For just a minute, let go of what you think you know. "Imagination is more important than knowledge," as Einstein profoundly articulated. We must learn to access and work with our imagination and go outside the proverbial nine dots. This is where the breakthroughs and the quantum growth exist. We don't have to force it, either. It really becomes a game of allowing the power of imagination to come to, or even through, us. It is our intuitive hits and flashes of brilliance that we must learn to nurture and advance.

So, how does one access this power and help others to do so? Asking questions unleashes the power of perspective that propels people to pivotal points of progress. However, to access the right questions, you must again surrender to curiosity and let go of what you think you already know. "Whoever undertakes to set himself up as a judge of Truth and Knowledge is shipwrecked by the laughter of the gods," according to Einstein. Let's face it, if you are reading this book, you are already successful on many levels. Wouldn't you agree that the more you know, the more you know you don't know?

To be a stellar coach is to not have all the answers but rather to be equipped with curiosity and powerful questions which can provoke the brilliance in the people you lead. Or as Einstein says, "The important thing is not to stop questioning. Curiosity has its own reason for existing." When you couple that statement with "Strive not to be a success, but rather to be of value," you can only come to realize that true impactful coaching is not imposing your answers or solutions on others, but rather seeing their brilliance and drawing it forth so they become empowered and accountable to their own purpose.

Trusting your intuition will set you apart as a valuable coach. Even Einstein said, "The only real valuable thing is intuition." Don't discount your experience and wisdom and knowledge of the right way to proceed or guide. This however, becomes a delicate dance of allowing those you are coaching to develop their wisdom by deriving from within rather than an injection from you.

Herein lies the difference between manager, mentor, leader and coach. There are obvious times where you must impart critical information to those you lead. You must share policy and procedure so they may operate accordingly and keep productivity and function unencumbered. However, when you are coaching, you are in the truest essence of people development. The reality of it is you can't do it for them. You can only provide the environment and feedback for them to allow their potential to unfold.

As a coach, remember these words Einstein told us, "Everything should be made as simple as possible, but not simpler." When you shift to coaching mode, avoid information overload and help them to navigate clear of overwhelm. It is conciseness and brevity which have the most impact to move people into action. According to Einstein, "Teaching should be such that what is offered is perceived as a valuable gift and not as a hard duty." The same can be said for coaching.

Any intelligent fool can make things bigger, more complex, and more violent. It takes a touch of genius - and a lot of courage - to move in the opposite direction. - Albert Einstein

Belief in self is paramount. Bridal your doubts, fears and anxieties, for those are the repellent of all desires, goals and achievements. Help those you coach bridal theirs as well. Identify and embrace your uniqueness, and show others how to do the same. We are meant to live our life and to serve others, not to live others' lives for them. When you suffer the attacks that may come from staying true to yourself, just remember the wisdom from one of the greatest minds the world has ever known, "Great spirits have always encountered violent opposition from mediocre minds."

When in doubt, simply remember these words which Einstein delivered in 1918 to the Physical Society, Berlin for Max Planck's sixtieth birthday, "The state of mind which enables a man to do work of this kind is akin to that of the religious worshiper or the lover; the daily effort comes from no deliberate intention or program, but straight from the heart."

It has taken one of the greatest minds to remind us that coaching is about coming from the heart.

Patti McKenna

Editor's Note

I love my job for various reasons, but one of the elements of my career as an editor that I like the most is that I get to meet and work with some rather impressive people. Machen MacDonald is one of those people. When I first talked with Machen regarding this book, it was my first official introduction to him, but not to his work. I was already familiar with Machen's business, articles, and, therefore, the personal and professional equation for success that he sets for himself as well as his clients. After completing this project, I find myself much more educated about coaching and informed about the dedication and commitment that the authors in this book hold for their work. They are experts in their field, and every profession, even an editor, can and will make tremendous strides in their success by following their blueprints and models. Thank you to Machen and the other esteemed authors in this book for sharing them with us.

www.ThePowerOfCoaching.com

Quick Order Form

The Power of Coaching
Engaging Excellence In Others
By Machen MacDonald
$14.95

Shipping: $2.50 for first book
$1.25 for each additional book
(California residents add 8.25% sales tax)

Fax Orders	Telephone Orders
Send this form to:	Call Toll Free:
530-687-8583	1-530-273-8000
	(Have your credit card ready)
Order On Line	
www.ThePowerOfCoaching.com	

Name _____

Address:_____

City/State/Zip:_____

Phone: _____

Email: _____

Method of Payment:

Visa   Master Card   American Express   Discover

Card Number: _____

Name on Card: _____

Expiration Date: _____

3-digit security code on back of card: _____

(If billing address is different from shipping address, please provide.)

Engaging Excellent Coaching Resources

To learn more about how to raise your game as a coach, be sure to visit with the authors of this book and their resources. Below are additional resources you may wish to explore:

International Coach Federation
2365 Harrodsburg Rd., Suite A325
Lexington, KY 40504
Phone: 888-423-3131
www.coachfederation.org

CoachVille
CoachVille LLC
PO Box 904
Hopatcong, NJ 07843
www.coachville.com

Professional Coaches and Mentors Association
800-768-6017
www.pcmaonline.com

Recommended reading list:
Visit   www.ThePowerOfCoaching.com